SPORTSPERFORMANCE

SWIMMING
GOING FOR STRENGTH AND STAMINA

SPORTSPERFORMANCE

SWIMMING
GOING FOR STRENGTH AND STAMINA

MARIANNE BREMS

CONTEMPORARY
BOOKS, INC.
CHICAGO ▪ NEW YORK

Library of Congress Cataloging-in-Publication Data

Brems, Marianne.
   Swimming—going for strength and stamina.

   (Sportsperformance)
   Bibliography: p.
   Includes index.
   1. Swimming.   2. Swimming—Training.   I. Title.
II. Series.
GV837.B796   1988   797.2'1'07   88-3570
ISBN 0-8092-4573-6 (pbk.)

Copyright © 1988 by Marianne Brems
All rights reserved
Published by Contemporary Books, Inc.
180 North Michigan Avenue, Chicago, Illinois 60601
Manufactured in the United States of America
Library of Congress Catalog Card Number: 88-3570
International Standard Book Number: 0-8092-4573-6

Published simultaneously in Canada by Beaverbooks, Ltd.
195 Allstate Parkway, Valleywood Business Park
Markham, Ontario L3R 4T8 Canada

Underwater photographs by Dave Gray
Abovewater photographs by Pat Bresee

To Theresa, who's just learning
the joys of swimming

CONTENTS

FOREWORD

Strength and *stamina*—these are words whose true meaning I know well. Through 20 years of four to six hours of daily training in the pool, I grew to understand and love the opportunity for the physical and mental exercise that comes from swimming.

Now I have made the necessary transition from swimming in order to be the best in the world to swimming in order to stay physically fit, emotionally sharp, and, to a certain extent, socially active. At this point in my life, the demands of work and travel have required me to adjust my concept of strength, stamina, and physical fitness. But I feel fortunate, as should anyone who cares about health, to remain involved in a structured program of lap swimming.

Marianne's book *Swimming: Going for Strength and Stamina* provides a cohesive basis for understanding the principles of swimming for fitness, including tips on how to reach a higher level of fulfillment and satisfaction from a swimming exercise regime. Marianne weaves a solid framework of easy-to-understand, step-by-step guidelines on stroke mechanics, training techniques, and workout structure. In addition, for each of the four strokes plus open water swimming, Marianne provides a wealth of fun and challenging workouts.

Plain and simple, *Swimming: Going for Strength and Stamina* offers a clear tutorial on obtaining proficiency and enjoyment from participation in swimming, and all from a teacher who practices what she preaches. I should know she does just that; each morning I attend swim practice, Marianne is there with me.

—Peter Rocca

ix

ACKNOWLEDGMENTS

No one stands alone in writing a book. Even though my name appears on the cover of this book, I am no exception.

I wish to sincerely thank Peter Rocca for taking time out of his busy schedule to write the Foreword. He has my respect not only for his lofty accomplishments as an Olympian, but also for continuing his swimming into his adult life.

For expert photography, I wish to thank Dave Gray and Pat Bresee, whose commitment to the project was indispensable. For photo printing, my appreciation goes to Katherine Kahrs Photography.

For appearing early one Sunday morning to have their stroke technique photographed, I extend my appreciation to Dick Ennis, Lane Looze, and Laura Val.

For patience, support, and input along the way, I am additionally grateful to Theresa Devonshire.

SPORTSPERFORMANCE

SWIMMING
GOING FOR STRENGTH AND STAMINA

INTRODUCTION

It would be a mistake to begin this book with the usual disclaimer about checking with a physician concerning the adequacy of your health for vigorous physical exercise. Not that this isn't important, but I'm assuming you know this, just as I'm assuming you know something about exercise in general. For example, this book does not tell you how to use heart-rate formulas as indicators of your level of exertion, since these formulas are available in any fitness guide. The book focuses instead on concepts and explanations that apply particularly to swimming and still more particularly to the swimmer who is serious about getting better. Suffice it to say that, perhaps because swimming is the ultimate low-impact aerobic, thanks to the cushioning effect of the water, or because it offers the essence of fitness—continuous exercise at an increased heart rate, I expect that you have already consulted with your physician about the sufficiency of your health and that you already own a swimsuit and a pair of goggles.

With this assumption in mind, it occurred to me that this book might aptly be called *The Streamlined Approach to Swimming* (pun intended). But that is exactly what I did; I streamlined my thinking on the subject of swimming. I asked myself, "What does a swimmer need to know when he

1

or she is through talking and ready to put in some time and effort?" And, as importantly, I asked, "What doesn't this swimmer need to know?" The answers to these questions resulted in the outline for this book.

But let me explain further. Of course, the techniques of the individual strokes, starts, and turns are important (and difficult to streamline because of the massive number of minute body movements that contribute to forward propulsion). But besides some lofty expositions of the perfect angle of the elbow and some snazzy shots of that new butterflylike breaststroke, I wanted to offer some down-to-earth practical drills that would allow you to learn through doing—experience being the best teacher, after all. Following these drills are workouts that bring together drills, stroke technique, and principles of training (explained in detail in Chapter 1) for a comprehensive presentation of each stroke. So thorough is the presentation that after you digest the material, you should be able to make up your own workouts.

Beyond technique, you may be interested in the concept of a swimming season, with its various phases. If you're working hard at improving (and that doesn't exclude fun), you probably won't want to train at the same intensity all the time. Furthermore, you may wish to plan a peak performance. Of course, it's OK if you don't want to think about competition now.

Concerning flexibility and strength training, I have addressed only exercises and equipment that apply to swimming. In addition to being in line with my philosophy for this book, this touches on one of the major advancements in swim training of the last five years. We live in a time of specialization in all aspects of life, and land strength training is no exception. The modern approach is therefore to duplicate with added resistance only those motions and at only those speeds which directly benefit swimming ability.

And then, voilà, you stand at the threshold of what might be considered an even higher experience, with the waves licking your toes. "Care for a swim across the lake?" the water invites. Why not, if you're properly prepared? And you will be if you follow the prescription in Chapter 9. It's an experience no pool can give you.

That brings us around to what I decided on your behalf you don't need to know right away. Since we already decided you have a suit, you certainly don't need to know what kind to get, or what kind you didn't get. Forget it. It's not important. I also thought a discussion on swimming injuries, few as they are, would be premature. For now just remember, if it hurts a lot, don't do it. You're supposed to be having fun, not tearing yourself down. As a precaution, however, don't go crazy with resistance devices too quickly. Finally, I left out variations on starting and turning techniques and other information I felt sure you would pick up from other swimmers in competition or from a coach.

For more information about organized competition, contact either of the following addresses:

Triathlon Federation
P.O. Box 1963
Davis, CA 94617-1963

Dorothy Donnelly
U.S. Masters Swimming
National Office
5 Piggott Lane
Avon, CT 06001

So with everything you need to know right at your fingertips, and none of the frills to slow you down, and with the motivation that caused you to buy your suit and goggles in the first place, give your muscles and joints a break from the stresses of gravity today. Swim to your heart's content.

1
PRINCIPLES OF TRAINING

The underlying principle we put our faith in when we train is that as we overload our bodies' cardiovascular systems, they will grow stronger to meet the increased demand. But clearly we must consider other principles as well, or we might quickly swim ourselves ragged and cause perhaps irreversible damage. The most basic of these principles is what I will call "the principle of efficiency," and several others will follow.

THE PRINCIPLE OF EFFICIENCY

We have all had the chance to observe the skilled and highly trained athlete perform and had the sense that the movements appeared so smooth and effortless that no exertion whatsoever was involved. I am reminded of Frank Shorter, who strode into the Olympic stadium in Munich to win the marathon and looked as if he had just combed his hair. By contrast, the sedentary office worker might appear to be close to cardiac arrest after merely climbing two flights of stairs.

To go the greatest possible distance with the lowest possible heart rate is only part of the total goal of training in swimming or any other aerobic sport. If this were the only objective, we would try to creep along at a snail's pace, conserving energy with every stroke, a technique that would bore even the most noncompetitive lap swimmer. But neither do we attempt the opposite. We don't, in our eagerness, tear madly and without method down the pool, making every move as difficult as possible solely to raise our level of exertion. The result would be almost instant exhaustion.

So what is the middle ground between the snail's pace and the helter-skelter styles of swimming? The answer is simple: it is efficiency, which implies a combination of greater speed and increased distance.

The next four chapters provide step-by-step points on efficient stroke technique for each of the four competitive swimming strokes. With a little study and some practice in the water, you'll be sure to improve. But even without stroke refinements, you'll become more efficient if you swim consistently, because you'll gain conditioning. The result is that you'll be able to go faster as well as farther while expending no more energy than before. (More on conditioning later in this section.) Therefore, to continue to benefit at the same level from your conditioning, you'll have to increase either your speed or your distance or both. Of course, increasing your speed is more time-efficient than adding distance.

TRAINING INTENSITY

In general, training affects our bodies by increasing our skill in the water and also by increasing the output of individual muscle fibers and allowing us to consume greater quantities of oxygen during exertion. All of these improvements supply us with more energy aerobically and significantly delay fatigue.

How does training do this? When the body's demand for blood and oxygen during prolonged and consistent periods of exercise are intense enough, increased aerobic endurance will develop. The key is the intensity, but not so much that it stays at a painfully high level on a consistent basis. Let me be clear that this is not the "no pain, no gain" theory of training. In fact, increases in oxygen consumption are more significant during endurance training than during sprint training, which is actually more intense. This is why, from the standpoint of fitness, we are encouraged to keep our heart rates at *continuously* elevated levels rather than to exercise with short bursts of energy.

The greatest training benefit of all is gained neither from long periods of low-intensity swimming nor from short all-out sprints. These may serve as part of a training program in varying degrees, depending upon whether endurance or speed is your primary goal, but more training benefit comes through interval training.

INTERVAL TRAINING

The term *interval training* refers to a series of periods of submaximal exercise alternating with controlled, short rest periods. The purpose of interval training is to reach a heart rate higher than that resulting from nonstop swimming and thus to build aerobic fitness. Brief rest periods in your workout should enable you to push your swims harder and thereby gain a higher level of fitness. The rests should be long enough to provide some rest but not long enough for your heart rate to drop significantly. Interval training is used by serious lap swimmers and competitive swimmers, and all of the workouts in this book are built around this concept.

Many of the exercises contained in these workouts involve repeating a number of identical or similar swims based on a fixed departure time, such as a set of eight 100-yard swims, beginning each 100-yard swim every 1 minute and 45 seconds (that is, 8 × 100 on 1:45). In most cases, I have added another time in parentheses following the fixed departure time, for example (:20), to indicate the intended approximate rest time should the departure interval be inappropriate for you.

Some of the other interval sets contained in the workouts are set up according to a fixed amount of rest. For example, for a set of eight 100s, the rest mights be indicated as "Rest

:20 between 100s." With this type of interval, the incentive to perform may be lower, since the rest time will be the same regardless of swimming time, but the emphasis may not always be on performance; rather it may be on stroke technique.

A rest "interval" can also exist in the form of a length or lengths of easy swimming or kicking interspersed between lengths of hard swimming or kicking, such as swimming 400 yards doing every third length at an easier pace. However, do not confuse this with swims in a series that begin with a moderate pace and "descend" to a faster pace. The technique of descending is used to develop the skill of even pacing.

Normally, rest intervals should not be long enough to allow your heart rate to drop to a nonworking rate; nevertheless, rest intervals vary in length depending upon the particular physiological process to be emphasized. As a general rule, interval training with short rest periods builds endurance and stamina more than speed and strength. Short rest intervals may be considered ones which are not greater than approximately $\frac{1}{6}$ of the swimming time. This represents a swim-to-rest ratio of 6:1; for example, possibly 10 × 75 yards with :10 rest between 75s. On the other hand, training with longer rest intervals builds speed more than endurance; for example, 10 × 75 yards with :30 rest between 100s, perhaps representing a 2:1 swim-to-rest ratio. In other words, when you do a set of 75 yard swims getting only :5 or :10 rest, the training effect is different than if you were to do the same set of 75 yard swims with :30 or :45 rest.

Interval training is highly versatile and efficient, and it is useful whether you're training for distance, sprints, or open water events. If you want to use interval training to prepare yourself for distances of 200 yards or more, spend at least 50 percent of your training session doing distances ranging from the length of the event to 100 percent longer, or shorter swims with a maximum of :10 rest, using a 6:1 swim-to-rest ratio. If you are a serious competitor, your pace should be as fast as you can make it without sacrificing consistency of speed throughout the set. The other 50 percent of your workout should include kicking, pulling, stroke drills, and shorter-distance, longer-rest swimming.

If you want to prepare for events of 100 yards or less, increase the number of sets consisting of shorter distances and longer rest, and decrease your swim-to-rest ratio for at least a few key sets each workout to 1:1 for 50s and 25s and to 2:1 for 100s, so that you can swim at near-maximum effort. Practice some swimming with limited breathing, but also keep up something of a distance base for conditioning purposes.

If you're using pool training to prepare for open water swimming, do as much as 75 to 80 percent distance swims, using distances of 50 to 100 percent of the race distance, depending upon how far you plan to swim in the open water. The remaining 20 to 25 percent should consist of kicking, pulling, and interval swimming with a 6:1 swim-to-rest ratio.

BASE TRAINING

Interval training should include a combination of "base training" and "specificity training." Base training lays a foundation, much like the foundation of a skyscraper, of strength and circulatory efficiency necessary for the faster, sharper, more specific training for particular swimming events.

Nort Thornton, in an article titled "Training for the Future," says that this foundation consists of long, slow distance swims plus shorter swims at a level of output well within the capacity of the swimmer but still requiring significant effort. No specific muscular adaptations take place during this type of training, but it has value for several reasons.

First, its effects are long lasting even through relatively long layoff periods or periods of considerably reduced training. This explains why a swimmer who has once built a base but has been out of the water for some months or even years may, if only temporarily, have an advantage over a less seasoned swimmer who is training regularly. But realize too that while the effects of base training last a relatively long time, consistency in your training program will offer the best overall results.

Second, the effects of base training can build themselves and improve continuously over the months and years. As in all walks of life, there's no substitute for experience.

Third, because the effects of base training cannot be achieved quickly and the pace of swimming during this phase is relatively slow, it provides an opportunity for relatively low physical and mental pressure.

Unfortunately base training, because of its very slowness, is compatible only to a certain degree with more specific kinds of training. This is the concept behind the early-season, midseason, and taper-training periods discussed in detail in Chapter 7. The reason for this incompatibility, according to Thornton, is that base training requires the body to have a large reserve of adaptation energy, which permits it to respond positively to changing physical demands, and hard, fast swimming tends to deplete this energy. As a general rule, several months of base training (depending upon your initial condition) is ideal before moving on to large amounts of specificity training.

SPECIFICITY TRAINING

Once you have laid a foundation of strength and circulatory efficiency, you can build muscular efficiency with some hard, fast swimming at race pace using relatively long rest periods as well as the specific stroke you want to specialize in. The key is to fine-tune the base you've already built, just as you would sharpen a knife that has already been created.

The value of this kind of training is precisely what its name implies: It can be specific for the exact capabilities required of a particular event, so that you can achieve amazing improvements in time within as little as six weeks. But by the same token, because of the exacting nature of this ability, you cannot maintain such a pinnacle of physiological efficiency nearly as long as the effects of a well-planned base training program—in fact, probably not more than three months at a time. This phenomenon is similar to a race car's need to be tweaked and tuned more often than the family sedan.

The pitfalls are that peak performance, despite the best laid plans, may not correspond to your exact preparation timetable. It may take a little bit more or a little bit less time than you anticipated, since there are always factors beyond your control, such as injury, illness, or environmental stresses. Some guesswork will always be involved. Also, because of the intensity of this type of training, you must take care to avoid energy depletion and overtraining, or a slump may result rather than a peak. The benefits, however, are far greater than with any other kind of training in use at present.

During specificity training, use the particular stroke that you wish to specialize in. You can use several strokes to lay a foundation and add variety to a workout, which is important, but if you're going to race in the breaststroke, you'd better work on the breaststroke. A good illustration of this point is that a national champion individual medley swimmer will surely not be a national champion in each of the individual strokes, simply because being the best requires specialization.

To help you specialize, the workouts in the stroke chapters of this book have been arranged not only to emphasize a particular stroke (with some attention given to variety), but also to emphasize speed or endurance so that you can practice specificity in the distance of your swims as well.

CONSISTENCY

Whether your goals for swimming are to maintain a high level of health and vigor, to enter and complete a triathlon, or to hone your body to maximum performance in the Nationals, your training methods and plan of action will take you only as far as your willingness to put forth consistent and persistent effort. Although this may sound rudimentary, it's as easy to let your swimming get crowded out of the day's schedule as it is to become hooked on the habit of pushing yourself too hard too often. Either way, you'll end up losing the major portion of the benefit to be gained, and very likely quitting altogether.

Pick a training schedule (consistent with your goals) that you can live with in the *long run,* even if everything else in your life doesn't go smoothly, because it won't. Above all, if you haven't already, learn to view the time you spend swimming as an investment in your own health and well-being. Then you'll treat it with the respect it deserves.

Realize, however, that if you don't swim at least three times a week, you can't call it fitness. At the other extreme, most of the adult competitors I know swim four to seven times a week, and younger swimmers of national caliber swim twice a day, usually six days a week. Clearly, the range of possibilities is broad, but again, choose a plan you can stick with.

Perhaps the best idea is to listen to your body and take a day off if you're feeling run-down. Of course, fatigue can be as much a result of life's other demands as of the stresses of swimming. If you're serious about your swimming, you may also find that you'll want to spend a few weeks or months preparing for a particular event or series of events, such as the open water swimming season. During this preparation, you might increase your training by as much as 50 percent, but for most swimmers, significant alterations either up or down in the overall yearly plan are short-lived. Remember: Choose a training schedule you can live with in the long run.

HOW MUCH?

The workouts contained in this book assume a relatively high level of conditioning and competence, considering that readers will have a wide range of ages and abilities. Some of you may want more, but if you do, you've probably had enough experience swimming to add on to what I've written from your own storehouse of workout exercises. Don't be discouraged if you are nowhere near swimming the amounts of the workouts in this book. They're meant for the skilled, and they're meant to grow with.

Since not only age and experience vary greatly, but also goals and interest, you may wish to use the following suggestions on reducing the yardage of a workout without disturbing its progression:

- If the distances of a set are short (100 yards or less), reduce the number of swims in the set. For example, change 10 × 100 yards to 6 × 100 yards.
- If the distances are long (more than 100 yards), reduce the distance. For example, change 3 × 300 yards to 3 × 200 yards.
- Of course, you can always change both if necessary.

Most Masters (adult) workouts last from an hour to an hour and a half, with some of the lap swimmers staying between a half-hour and an hour. If you swim on your own, you may have more flexibility. If you have been out of the water for an extended period or are just starting, you might not want to swim two or more days in a row at first. You'll know by listening to your body (a good idea in any case).

GOAL SETTING AND MOTIVATION

As in any good business plan, the first and by far most important prerequisite to determining how you'll spend your time productively is to establish where you're starting and where you want to end up. When setting a goal, I prefer to focus initially on what I really want. Nothing else. It's difficult to keep out thoughts about how far away the goal seems, how much work it's going to take to get there, or—worst of all—how impossible the goal is for any of a hundred reasons, but sometimes these thoughts are necessary for the purpose of finding something that is properly motivating. Once that's done and clear in my mind, then and only then am I ready to think about where I'm starting.

Most often in competitive swimming, the goal takes the form of completing a certain distance within a certain time. In this case, you must determine how fast you are initially, and then set intermediate goals, trying to drop your times bit by bit in practice for sets of that distance or near that distance. Some of the workouts, particularly the ones in the taper section, include "broken" swims (swims with short rest intervals inserted). These are intended to give you an idea of how fast you can swim under race conditions. Since practice times will be slower than meet times, the rest during a broken swim is added to make up for the lack of freshness. The result is times that are surprisingly close to race times. For example, if you swim 200 yards in practice, resting :10 at each 50-yard increment, you will very likely find that your swimming time is close to your time for the 200-yard event in a meet.

When it comes to adjusting your game plan or achieving the next goal that you set, a good reference tool is a log book in which you keep track of these practice times along with a record of each day's workout. Let's say that after a time, you're progressing toward your goal more slowly than you'd like to. (This probably happens most of the time, but frequently it's impatience rather than a flaw in your training.) At this point, you can use your log book to go back to the sequence of workouts leading up to that time. Ask yourself questions like these: Am I doing enough distance? Am I increasing speed when I should be? Am I doing enough sprinting? Am I doing enough of the specific stroke or strokes that I want to specialize in? Then you can make changes if necessary, or if you have a coach, you can discuss your observations with him or her.

Your log book can become an even more valuable resource if you make notes next to your workouts as to how you felt physically and mentally during the different portions of the workout—where you felt strong, where you felt not so strong, if you felt sore, and if you felt as if you were coming down with an illness. This will help you tune in to your body and foresee times when you should perhaps back off for a day or two or more.

The most motivating experience for anyone in any endeavor is the progressive realization of worthwhile goals.

For this reason, goal setting and motivation always go hand in hand. But life will be life in swimming as in anything else, and there will be times when you will feel you are not progressing toward your goals, or when your goals are less specific and demanding. At these times, it's motivating just to remember how swimming burns up calories and fats, increases oxygen consumption, and strengthens your cardiovascular system, all of which increase your energy and probably your lifespan as well.

2
FREESTYLE

Probably the most modern concept of stroke mechanics in swimming is that the thrust that propels a swimmer's body through the water is at least as much a result of lift as of drag. Avoiding a long discussion of hydrodynamics, this simply means that when you perform a swimming stroke, the upward and downward and inward and outward movements of your hands and feet contribute significantly to the effectiveness of the stroke. Previously, it had been thought that the only way to move forward in the water was to push directly backward against the resistance of the water. Think of your hands and feet as propellers rather than oars.

How does this translate into movements in the water? Let us begin by looking at the armstroke.

ARMSTROKE

The armstroke consists of a hand entry, a catch, a downsweep, an insweep, an upsweep, and a recovery, all of which flow together in one continuous motion. Together, these elements of the armstroke are designed to create the maximum propulsion through use of the lift force and minimum resistance through streamlining.

Your fingertips should enter the water first, with the palm turned slightly to the outside. The entry should be at a

16

point somewhere between a line extending forward from the middle of your head and another extending forward from the tip or your shoulder on the same side. Your hand should slice into the water about 8-10 inches before complete arm extension and should continue forward just below the surface of the water.

Once you have completely extended your arm, you'll begin the catch by flexing the wrist downward and outward, and you begin to exert pressure against the water at precisely the moment that the arm on the other side leaves the water.

The downsweep then takes place. The hand, which should be ahead of the elbow, moves downward, and the elbow begins to bend. At the completion of the downsweep, the head is almost directly over the hand.

During the insweep, the hand angles in to the midline of the body, and the elbow reaches maximum bend (approximately 90 degrees). At this point, the hand is accelerating, and the shoulders travel past the hand. During the upsweep, the hand pushes almost directly backward while it is still accelerating. As the arm fully extends, the palm rotates inward so the little finger slides out of the water first.

The elbow comes up and remains high throughout recovery. Roll your body enough to allow the forearm to hang relaxed so that the fingertips travel forward near the surface.

KICK

Slight lateral movements of the legs occur during kicking if ankle flexibility is good. This is preferable to kicking straight up and down, again because of the lift force that's created.

Ankle flexibility is the key to efficient kicking because the more fully you can extend your ankles, the greater the surface area of the foot available to exert pressure against the water. (See Chapter 8 for exercises to increase ankle flexibility.) Kicking originates at the hips, so the knees bend only slightly on the downbeat and are straight on the up-

The catch

The beginning of the downsweep

The end of the
downsweep

The insweep

The upsweep

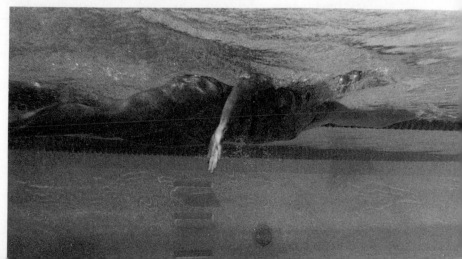

beat. The kicks are small, since the distance between the feet when they are farthest apart should not be more than 12–16 inches. Only the heels break the surface, not the whole foot.

Many swimmers use a six-beat kick, that is, six downward kicks (three with each foot) for every complete arm cycle (right and left arms). Some, however, prefer a two-beat kick, which has only two downward kicks (one with each foot) for every complete arm cycle. A six-beat kick creates more power but also require more energy, so it is well suited to sprinting. A two-beat kick, by similar logic, is perhaps best suited for distance swimming. However, it is a rare individual indeed who can change from one to the other when going from sprint to distance swimming or vice versa. Usually a swimmer feels more comfortable with one or the other and will stick to that.

BODY POSITION AND BREATHING

When considering body position, realize that streamlining is of the utmost importance. Clearly, a body parallel to the surface as it moves along encounters less resistance than one at an angle. For that reason, the feet should not drop much below the shoulders. To accomplish this, keep the kicks small and the waterline at about the hairline.

Breathing also plays a significant role in maintaining a horizontal body position. You must roll your head to the side for inhalation, since lifting it tends to make the feet sink lower in the water. You need not turn it far to get a quick breath before returning to a face-down position for exhalation. Be sure to breathe in and out completely.

QUICK CHECKLIST
Underwater Armstroke
1. Fingertips enter first.
2. Palm turns out.
3. Hand enters between head and shoulder.
4. Hand enters 8–10 inches before complete extension.

5. Hand stretches forward.
6. Wrist flexes downward and outward.
7. Hand moves downward.
8. Elbow bends.
9. Hand angles to midline.
10. Elbow reaches maximum bend.
11. Hand accelerates.
12. Hand pushes back.
13. Palm rotates inward.

Arm Recovery
1. Elbow is high.
2. Body rolls.
3. Forearm is relaxed.

Kick
1. Kick from hips.
2. Bend knee slightly on downbeat.
3. Keep knee straight on upbeat.
4. Use small kicks.
5. Keep feet 12–16 inches apart.
6. Heels break surface.
7. Choose six-beat kick or two-beat kick.

Body Position and Breathing
1. Streamline.
2. Keep body parallel to surface.
3. Keep waterline at hairline.
4. Head rolls to side.
5. Head turns short distance.
6. Inhale and exhale completely.

FREESTYLE MINICLINIC*

It's always fun to break your regular swimming routine a bit by throwing in something besides your basic kicking, pulling, and swimming. How about some stroke drills that not only break monotony, but serve to point out to you cer-

*"Freestyle Mini-Clinic" adapted with permission of *Swim* magazine, P.O. Box 45497, Los Angeles, CA 90045

tain stroke defects you may not even know you have? But you won't be left hanging (floating?!)—these drills will also help you to correct whatever imperfections you may find. When done in order, the drills provide quite a thorough rehearsal of stroke techniques, but you may do them individually as needed.

In concentrating particularly on your kick in the first three stroke drills, consider the following characteristics of an efficient kick:

- Ankles are relaxed.
- Feet are at the same level as shoulders.
- Kicks are small.
- Kicks originate from hips, not knees.
- Only heels break the surface.

Stroke Drill 1—Sit as close to the edge of the pool as possible, letting your legs dangle in the water. Slowly move your feet up and down, keeping your knees straight but not stiff and your ankles as loose as possible. Be sensitive to the feeling of the water pressing your toes down as you push each leg up, since this is the motion that creates propulsion. You can heighten the sensation of this drill by doing it wearing a pair of swim fins.

Stroke Drill 2—Put one hand on the gutter or coping of the pool and the other hand on the pool wall a foot or so below the surface. Extend your body on the surface, stomach down. Freestyle kick from your hips down so that your heels break the surface and your feet come apart vertically 12-16 inches. With your head above water, you will be able to hear from the turbulence or lack of it if your kick is too low or too high. Again, be aware of the pressure of the water against your toes. This drill will help you to develop a feel for the kick without distractions.

Stroke Drill 3—Extend your left arm under your left ear and your right arm along your right side. Kick in this position with your body rolled one-quarter of a turn to the right side. Repeat the drill while extending your right arm under your right ear and rolling your body to the left side.

The remaining freestyle stroke drills are designed most importantly to develop proper armstroke and body position. In practicing these drills, keep in mind the following characteristics of an efficient pull:

- The most effective armstroke is one that carries you the maximum distance per stroke.
- Hand entry is between a point in front of the shoulder and one in front of the head.
- Each arm extends all the way forward underwater.
- Opposite arm extends all the way to the rear.
- Elbows are high during recovery.
- Each hand follows a pattern of downsweep, insweep, and upsweep.

Stroke Drill 4—Hold a kickboard on the bottom edge with one hand (elbow straight), and swim freestyle with the opposite arm, making sure to extend the stroking arm as far forward as possible under the board. This will help you learn the proper hand entry position, since you will be prevented from crossing over too far. You will also have the opportunity to practice extending your stroke. Be sure to do the drill on both right and left sides.

Stroke Drill 5—Same as Stroke Drill 4, only take one stroke with the right arm, then one with the left, and so on in a normal swimming pattern. Here you lose your chance to extend your stroke, but you can practice correct hand entry and concentrate on one arm at a time.

Stroke Drill 6—Same as Stroke Drill 4, only one arm is extended without a kickboard. This gives you less support and is slightly more difficult than with a board. But at the same time it's more like regular swimming.

Stroke Drill 7—Same as Stroke Drill 5, except that no board is used. This drill will be referred to as "catch-up."

Stroke Drill 8—Hold a short stick or baton (six to eight inches long) in your left hand as you take a freestyle stroke with your right arm. When your right arm returns to the forward position, switch the baton to your right hand and complete a stroke with your left arm. This drill will be referred to as "baton."

Stroke Drill 9—Swim freestyle by extending one arm in front of the same shoulder and letting the other arm relax along your side for a count of six kicks; then switch arm positions by taking a regular stroke for six more kicks. Continue switching, trying to make your arms feel as long and stretched out as possible.

Stroke Drill 10—Same as Stroke Drill 9, but count only four kicks.

Stroke Drill 11—Same as Stroke Drill 9, but count only three kicks. (This is the normal swimming pattern with a six-beat kick. You should have no hesitation here.)

Stroke Drill 12—Count the number of arm cycles needed to swim one length of the pool. Repeat, trying to extend your arms in the forward and backward positions as much as possible, but keeping your arms constantly moving. Try to reduce the number of strokes needed.

Stroke Drill 13—Swim freestyle, dragging your fingertips through the water on the recovery. This technique is very useful in helping you get your elbows high and your forearms relaxed during recovery. This drill will be referred to as "ripple."

Stroke Drill 14—Swim directly above a black line on the bottom of the pool. Follow with your eyes the path that your hand makes until it passes too far under your body to be seen. Observe your hand traveling downward and then sweeping in toward the black line. You will see better if you use goggles during this drill.

Stroke Drill 15—Swim freestyle, making your hands into fists instead of keeping your palms flat as you would normally do. You'll feel the lost resistance. This drill will be referred to as "fists."

Stroke Drill 16—Swim freestyle, breathing alternately on the right side and then on the left side during the next stroke. Practicing this technique will help you gain stroke balance. This drill will be referred to as "alternate breathing."

The final two freestyle stroke drills are designed for additional thorough work on lengthening your stroke and understanding the concept of maximum distance per stroke.

Stroke Drill 17—Do a dog paddle stroke combining exaggerated body roll with very long strokes.

Stroke Drill 18—Tie a piece of ordinary rope or nylon line to the eye where a lane line fastens. (The lane line should be removed.) If the rope is long enough, attach it somewhat tightly at the other end of the pool; if not, let one end go free in the water. Position yourself above the rope and parallel to it, grabbing the rope below you one hand at a time and pulling yourself along. Unfortunately, your propulsion here is limited to backward motions to the exclusion of lateral and up-and-down motions, but the principle of pulling yourself past a nearly stationary point is sound enough. Remember to make each pull as long as you can. Don't forget an over-the-water recovery and a proper kick.

WORKOUTS

The next five workouts are designed to help you develop speed in freestyle.

WORKOUT 1*

Distance	Stroke	Time
200	Free Pick up pace as distance decreases	Warm-up
150	Free pull with buoy**	
100	Free kick	
50	Free	
10 × 50	Free Baton**	Rest :10 after each 50
5 × 100	Free Descend**	On 1:30 (:15)
50	Choice of strokes Easy	
4 × 100	Free #1–#3: easy #2–#4: fast	On 1:40 (:25)
50	Choice of strokes Easy	
3 × 100	Free Very fast	On 1:50 (:35)
50	Choice of strokes	
2 × 200	I.M.** kick 25 no board kick, 25 swim	Rest :20 between 200s
4 × 50	Free kick	On 1:00
4 × 25	Free Head-out**	On :30
4 × 25	Free No breath	On :30
8 × 25	Free Odd numbers easy Even numbers fast	On :25
100	Free	Swim-down

3,450　yards total

*Note that all workouts in this book are geared to a 25-yard pool simply
because this is the most common type of facility. If you train in a meter pool,
multiply time intervals by 1.1 or add 5 seconds per 50 meters, 10 seconds per
100 meters, and so on.

**See Glossary.

WORKOUT 2

Distance	Stroke	Time
400	I.M.	Warm-up
	Substitute free for fly	
4 × 100	Free	Rest :10 after each
	25 Stroke Drill 9	100
	25 Stroke Drill 10	
	50 Stroke Drill 11	
3 × { 100	Free	Rest :5 per 25 at end
75	Increase speed as distance	of each distance
50	decreases	
25	Descend sets 1–3	
25	Free pull with buoy, paddles*,	Rest :5 per 25 at the
50	and tube*	end of each
75		distance
100		
100		
75		
50		
25		
5 × 50	Free	On :55 (:20)
5 × 50		On :50 (:15)
5 × 50		On :45 (:10)
5 × 50		On :55 (:20)
100	Choice of strokes kick	Rest :5 per 25 at the
75		end of each
50		distance
100	Free	Swim-down

3,400	yards total

*See Glossary.

27

WORKOUT 3

Distance	Stroke	Time
10:00	Choice of strokes	Warm-up
4 × 150	Free 25 catch-up*, 25 normal, 25 ripple, 25 normal, 25 fists*, 25 normal	Rest :15 between 150s
4 × 100	Free Very fast	Rest 1:00 between 100s
6 × 75	Kick 50 your specialty, 25 free	On 1:30
6 × 75	Free Accelerate through each 75	On 1:15 (:15)
? × 50	Free	Begin on 1:15 and decrease interval by :5 on each swim until failure at interval
8 × 50	Free pull with buoy, paddles and tube Work on fast turnover	On :50 (:10)
8 × 50	Free with fins Work on fast turnover	On :40
200	Free	Swim-down

2,900 yards + 10:00 swim + ? × 50 yards total

*See Glossary.

28

WORKOUT 4

Distance	Stroke	Time
500	Free 25 right arm, 25 left arm, 25 catch-up, 25 ripple Repeat × 5	Warm-up
10 × 50	25 choice of strokes, 25 Free 2nd 25 fast than 1st	On :50 (:10)
2 × 200	Free broken*	Rest :10 between each 50, 1:00 between 200s
2 × 300	Free 25 breathe every 3 strokes 25 breathe every 5 strokes 25 breathe every 7 strokes 25 breathe every 9 strokes Repeat × 3	Rest :30 between 300s
4 × 100	Free broken #1: No break #2: Rest :20 at 50s #3: Rest :10 at 25s #4: Rest :10 at 25s (#4 faster than #3)	Rest 1:00 between 100s
15 × 50	Free pull 5 with buoy, paddles, and tube 5 with buoy and paddles 5 with buoy	On :50 (:10)
5 × 100	#1: I.M. #2: 25 back, 25 breast, 25 free, 25 fly #3: 25 breast, 25 free, 25 fly, 25 back #4: 25 free, 25 fly, 25 back, 25 breast	On 1:40 (:20)
20 × 25	Kick 5 free 10 choice of strokes 5 free	On :30
100	Free	Swim-down

4,250 yards total

*See Glossary.

WORKOUT 5

Distance	Stroke	Time
8 × 50	Choice of strokes Alternate 50 kick, 50 swim	Warm-up
8 × 75	Free Build speed through each 75	Rest :15 between 75s
8 × 100	Free Descend #1–4, #5–8 #8 fast than #4	4 on 1:30 (:20) 4 on 1:20 (:10)
50	Free pull with buoy, paddles, and tube Breathe every 3 strokes	Rest :5 per 25 after each distance
100	Breathe every 5 strokes	
150	Breathe every 7 strokes	
200	Breathe every 9 strokes	
150	Breathe every 7 strokes	
100	Breathe every 5 strokes	
50	Breathe every 3 strokes	
4 × 100	Free 25 head-out sprint 75 easy	On 1:40 (:15)
400	I.M. kick Increase speed from 1st to 4th 25 for each stroke	
10 × 12½	Free Sprint faster than best 25 time divided by 2	On :30
5:00	Practice dives	
200	Free	Swim-down

3,725   + 5:00 practice on dives total

The next five workouts are designed to help you develop endurance in freestyle.

WORKOUT 6

Distance	Stroke	Time
600	Free	Warm-up
	100 right arm	
	100 left arm	
	100 Stroke Drill 17	
	100 Stroke Drill 9	
	100 Stroke Drill 10	
	100 Stroke Drill 11	
3 × 200	Free pull with buoy, paddles, and tube	On 3:00 (:30)
800	Free	Rest :30 between
	Check time at 600 to beat on next swim	swims
600	Check time at 400	
400	Check time at 200	
200	All out	
300	I.M. kick	Rest :20 between
200	Free kick	each distance
100	I.M. kick	
100	Free	Swim-down
3,900	yards total	

WORKOUT 7

Distance	Stroke	Time
8:00	Free, choice Alternate breathing* Choice of strokes every 4th 25	Warm-up
400	Free, Negative split*	Rest :30 after each
2 × 100	Fly, Descend	free distance, :15
300	Free, Negative split*	after 2 × 100
2 × 100	Back, Descend	
200	Free, Negative split	
2 × 100	Breast, Descend	
100	Free, Negative split	
800	Free pull with buoy, paddles, and tube	
800	Free Descend by 200s, keeping stroke count on each length consistent	
400	Free kick Alternate 25 hard, 25 easy	

3,600 yards   + 8:00 swim total

*See Glossary.

WORKOUT 8

Distance	Stroke	Time
200	Free kick	Warm-up
200	Free pull with buoy	
200	Free swim	
16 × 100 + 50	Free Hold even pace	On average 100 pace during 1,650 swim + :15
400	I.M. kick No board 2nd 50 of each 100	
16 × 50	Free	4 on :50 (:10) 4 on :45 (:5) 4 on :40 (<:5) 4 on :50 (:10)
400	Free pull with buoy, paddles, and tube Breast every 4th 25	
100	Free	Swim-down

3,950   yards total

WORKOUT 9

Distance	Stroke	Time
500	Free	Warm-up
	100 Stroke Drill 12	
	100 normal	
	100 baton	
	100 normal	
	100 Stroke Drill 12	
6 × 125	Pull with buoy, paddles, and tube	On 1:45 (:10)
	75 free, 50 choice	
500	Free	On 6:15 (:30)

		Stroke	Time
	:45	Free kick: Hard	
	:15	Easy	
3 ×	:30	Hard	
	:15	Easy	
	:15	Hard	
	:15	Easy	

Distance	Stroke	Time
500	Free broken	Rest :10 at 100s
	For time	
100	Free	Swim-down
3,350	yards + 6:45 kick total	

WORKOUT 10

Distance	Stroke	Time
400	Free Alternate breathing Count strokes every 4th 25 Keep count consistent for even pace	Warm-up
400	Free Get time at 300 to beat on next swim	Rest :30 between swims
300	Get time at 200	
200	Get time at 100	
100	Very fast	
1,000	Free pull with buoy, paddles, and tube 100 breathe every 3 strokes 100 breathe every 5 strokes 100 breathe every 7 strokes 100 breathe every 9 strokes 100 breathe every 11 strokes Repeat × 2	
? × 100	Free Do 100s until failure at interval, then do 2 more on last interval made	Best time for 100 + :40 = 1st interval Subtract :5 more on each subsequent interval
400	I.M. kick Descend 1st–4th 25 of each stroke	
200	Free	Swim-down
3,000	yards + ? × 100 yards total	

3
BACKSTROKE

As with the freestyle, the lift theory of propulsion plays a significant role in creating an efficient backstroke. In fact, despite some obvious physiological limitations in the human shoulder joint, the freestyle and the backstroke are surprisingly similar with regard to the directions in which the arms and legs exert pressure upon the water. The backstroke's advantage over all the other strokes is that it requires no compromises in stroke mechanics to allow for breathing.

ARMSTROKE

The armstroke consists of a hand entry, a catch, a first downsweep, an upsweep, a second downsweep, and a recovery, which flow together in one motion. The hands never stop moving or propulsion and momentum would be lost and speed would decrease.

When you begin the stroke, your arm is fully extended in a line directly behind the shoulder on the same side. Your hand is also in line and is turned palm out so that the little finger is the first part to enter the water.

During the catch, your wrist will bend slightly, causing the hand to move forward, downward, and outward with the palm facing downward and outward.

35

The beginning of the upsweep

The end of the upsweep

The beginning of the second downsweep

The downsweep

The late downsweep

At this point, your arm begins to follow your hand in a downward and outward sweeping motion until the hand is about 18 inches deep. As this takes place, hand speed is increasing while the shoulder on the opposite side comes up out of the water and your hips roll toward the downsweep.

As downsweep becomes upsweep, the hand pushes slightly outward before the palm, with fingers pointing away from the body, begins pushing upward and then backward. During the upsweep, the elbow reaches its maximum bend (about 90 degrees).

The second downsweep begins as your hand rounds a curve at the top of the upsweep and starts pushing downward and inward to complete the final portion of the S-shaped pattern. At the end, your arm is completely extended, and your hand is below the level of your thigh.

To begin the recovery, your palm turns inward so the thumb emerges first as the extended arm and shoulder come up out of the water. Your hand travels in an arc directly above the shoulder on the same side.

KICK

As in the freestyle, the key to efficient kicking in the backstroke is ankle flexibility. A wide range of motion allows you to more fully use the surface area of your feet. Also as in the freestyle, kicking is from the hips, not the knees. But in the backstroke, the upbeat rather than the downbeat is the power phase of the kick. Therefore, the knees bend slightly on the upbeat but remain straight on the downbeat. Keep in mind that the feet follow an up-and-down motion, not a cyclical pattern with knees breaking the surface. The distance between the feet when they are farthest apart is only 12–16 inches. Only your toes break the surface, giving the water the appearance of boiling. Turning your toes slightly inward will offer an improved angle for propulsion.

A six-beat kick is used in the backstroke, since it has a greater stabilizing effect than a two-beat kick. Because each arm extends upward a relatively great distance above the body during recovery, you need the balancing effect of a strong kick.

BODY POSITION AND BREATHING

The proper body position in the backstroke is a happy medium between carrying the hips high in the water so as to avoid excessive resistance and carrying the hips low so that the knees do not break the surface.

Body position is largely determined by head position. The head is properly situated when the ears are barely submerged and the waterline is at the middle of the head and just below the chin. To maintain this position, keep your eyes focused on an object approximately 45 degrees from the surface, and do not allow your head to move up and down or from side to side.

Although head motions are not required for breathing, you must establish a breathing pattern so that you inhale and exhale completely. A good strategy is to start your inhalation when one hand breaks the surface to begin recovery and to start your exhalation when the other hand emerges to begin recovery.

QUICK CHECKLIST

Underwater Armstroke
1. Stroke is continuous.
2. Arm is in line with shoulder.
3. Bend wrist with palm facing downward and outward.
4. Arm moves downward and outward.
5. Hand begins to accelerate.
6. Hand pushes outward.
7. Hand pushes upward, then outward.
8. Elbow bend is 90 degrees.
9. Hand pushes downward and inward.
10. Arm extends below thigh level.

Arm Recovery
1. Thumb emerges first.
2. Arm and shoulder roll out of water.
3. Arc of hand is above shoulder.

Kick
1. Kick from hips.

39

2. Bend knee slightly on the upbeat.
3. Keep knee straight on downbeat.
4. Foot motion is up and down.
5. Feet are 12–16 inches apart.
6. Toes break surface.
7. Toes turn in.
8. Use six-beat kick.

Body Position and Breathing
1. Hips ride near surface.
2. Waterline is at middle of head and just below chin.
3. Eyes focus at 45 degrees.
4. Head does not move.
5. Inhale and exhale completely.

BACKSTROKE MINICLINIC*

To evaluate and fine-tune your stroke efficiency, review the following list of objectives, and use the program of progressive stroke drills intended to help you reach those objectives. Following the suggestions here will give you an understanding of some of the key points of efficient backstroke swimming as well as the particular level of your development, even without the help of a coach.

Let's begin by considering the kick and how it relates to body position. An efficient kick has these characteristics:

- Ankles are relaxed.
- Feet are at the same level as the hips and head.
- Kicks are small.
- Toes turn in.
- Toes are the only part of the foot to break the surface.
- You should feel 10 feet tall.

Stroke Drill 19—Sit as close to the edge of the pool as possible, dangling your legs in the water. Kick your legs slowly

*"Backstroke Mini-Clinic" adapted with permission from *Swim* magazine, P.O. Box 45497, Los Angles, CA 90045.

up and down, keeping your ankles as loose as possible and your knees straight. This will give you a feel for the water pressing your toes down during the propulsive phase of your kick. You can heighten the sensation of this drill by doing it wearing a pair of fins.

In the following drill, keep your chin high, keep your kicks shallow, turn your toes slightly inward for maximum leverage, and stretch out your body in the water as much as possible. This will help streamline your body in a level position with regard to the surface of the water.

Stroke Drill 20—Kick on your back with your arms extended behind your head, squeezing your ears, and your hands clasped together. Glance at your feet and legs periodically to see that only your toes break the surface—*not* your whole foot and *not* your knees. Your knees should be straight but not stiff, and your elbows should be locked. Try to feel like you're 10 feet tall.

If you can do the following drill for a length of the pool without getting water in your face, then you can be pretty certain that your body position and propulsion are good.

Stroke Drill 21—Kick on your back with one arm extended behind your shoulder, the other arm extended straight up at a 90-degree angle to your body.

With good body position already established, improving your armstroke is much easier. In building your skills in this area, consider these characteristics of an efficient pull:

- Arms keep moving so they remain opposite one another.
- Shoulders roll out of the water.
- Arms are straight on recovery.
- Hands enter behind the shoulders.
- Elbows bend 90 degrees underwater.
- Pull ends with palms facing down.

Sometimes backstrokers form the habit of completing a full arm cycle with one arm before starting the arm cycle with the other arm. In other words, each arm hesitates between the end of the pull and the beginning of the recovery, so that at one point in the stroke no propulsion is coming from either arm. The following three drills can help eliminate such hesitation.

Stroke Drill 22—Swim backstroke by extending one arm behind the same shoulder and letting the other arm relax at your side for a count of six kicks. Then switch arm positions for six more kicks. Keep switching.

Stroke Drill 23—Same as Stroke Drill 22, but count only four kicks.

Stroke Drill 24—Same as Stroke Drill 22, but count only three kicks. This is the normal swimming pattern. You should have no hesitation here.

Shoulder roll is also important for maximum efficiency. It helps to get a good catch on the water with your pulling arm and get your shoulder out of the water for lowered resistance on the recovery arm.

Stroke Drill 25—Backstroke with one arm, the other arm at your side with the shoulder raised above the surface when the opposite arm is underwater.

Once your shoulder roll has sent your pulling arm approximately 18 inches deep, your elbow comes in close to your body and bends up to 90 degrees for maximum leverage. Most swimmers need to bend more. The motion is somewhat similar to throwing a ball at your feet.

Stroke Drill 26—Backstroke with one arm, the other arm at your side, your stroking arm as close to a lane line as possible. As you begin your pull, grab the bottom of the lane line or one of the floats and push yourself along all the way to the end of the stroke. At the beginning of each stroke, make sure your hand enters the water right on top of the lane line so you know you're not crossing over behind your head. Also, watch to see that your recovery is with a straight arm.

Stroke Drill 27—Same as Stroke Drill 26, but stroke with both arms, trying to simulate the motion of the arm on the line with the arm away from the line. Be sure to complete each stroke by finishing in a palms-down position for maximum distance per stroke.

Stroke Drill 28—Cross your ankles and pull backstroke with no flotation devices. This will force you to finish your stroke.

As a final self-evaluation, check your technique with three last drills.

Stroke Drill 29—This drill helps you develop an accurate perception of how the surface of your palms works (or doesn't work) as propellers. Backstroke, making your hands into fists rather than keeping your palms flat. You'll feel the lost resistance.

Stroke Drill 30—Increase your resistance by stretching out your stroke as much as possible, rolling properly, and fully completing each stroke. Backstroke, counting the number of strokes you need to swim one length of the pool. Repeat the drill several times, trying to reduce the number of strokes on each attempt. Your arms must keep moving.

If you succeed at these two drills and can keep your head still on top of it, you may truly consider yourself an accomplished backstroker. Check the stability of your head position with the following drill.

Stroke Drill 31—Backstroke with a hand paddle resting on your forehead. See if you can complete at least two lengths of the pool without having to replace it.

WORKOUTS

The next five workouts are designed to help you develop speed in the backstroke.

WORKOUT 11

Distance	Stroke	Time
400	I.M. reverse order 50 kick, 50 swim each stroke	Warm-up
8 × 50	Back 2 normal 2 Stroke Drill 22 2 Stroke Drill 23 2 Stroke Drill 24	On :50 (:10)
16 × 25	Kick Alternate 25 back, 25 choice of strokes	On :30
12 × 100	Back For each set of 4: #1: 25 kick, 75 swim #2: 25 swim, 25 kick, 50 swim #3: 50 swim, 25 kick, 25 swim #4: 75 swim, 25 kick	4 on 1:30 (:10) 4 on 1:25 (:5) 4 on 1:20 (<:5)
200	Choice of strokes pull with buoy, paddles, and tube Increase speed as distance decreases	Rest :20 between swims

4 × { 75
50
25
	Back
	  Increase speed as distance
	  decreases
		Rest :15 between
		swims

100	Choice of strokes	Swim-down
3,300	total yards	

WORKOUT 12

Distance	Stroke	Time

500	Back
	  100 swim
	  100 kick
	  100 right arm
	  100 left arm
	  100 swim
		Warm-up

12 × 50	Around-the-walls 50s*
	  #1–3: fly
	  #4–6: back
	  #7–9: breast
	  #10–12: free
		On :50 (:10)

4 × { 100 / 2 × 50 / 4 × 25	Back
	  Very fast
		Rest :30 between
		  swims

5 × 100	Choice of strokes pull with buoy, paddles, and tube	On 1:30 (:15)
5 × 100	I.M. kick	On 2:00
10 × 25	Back Alternate 25 hard, 25 easy	On :25 (:10)
100	Free	Swim-down
3,650	yards total	

*See Glossary.

WORKOUT 13

Distance	Stroke	Time
600	100 free	Warm-up
	100 free pull with buoy	
	100 free side kick*	
	100 choice of strokes	
	100 choice of strokes pull with buoy	
	100 choice of strokes side kick	
4 × 25	Back sprint: With fins	On :20
4 × 100	Back: With fins	On 1:20 (:15)
4 × 25	Back sprint: With paddles	On :25
4 × 100	Back: With paddles	On 1:30 (:15)
4 × 25	Back Sprint	On :25
4 × 100	Back	On 1:30 (:15)
8 × 75	Choice of strokes pull	On 1:20 (:15)
	With choice of equipment	
8 × 75	Kick	On 1:30 (:15)
	25 fly, 25 back, 25 breast	
2 × 200	Back: broken	Rest 2:00 between
	#1: Rest :20 at 100	200s
	#2: Rest :10 at 50s	
100	Free	Swim-down

3,800   yards total

*See Glossary.

WORKOUT 14

Distance	Stroke	Time
100	Free	Warm-up
4 × 25	Back pull with legs crossed (no buoy)	
100	Free	
4 × 25	Back Stroke Drill 21	
100	Free	
20 × 50	Back	5 on :50 (:15) 5 on :45 (10) 5 on :40 (:5) 5 on :50 (:15)
5 × 100	Choice of strokes pull	Rest :15 between 100s
? × 50	Back Do 100s until failure at interval, then do 2 more on last interval made	Best time for 50 + :40 = 1st interval Subtract :5 more on each subsequent interval
5 × 100	I.M.	On 1:40 (:20)
15 × 12½	Back Sprint at faster than best 25 time divided by 2	On :30
10 × 25	Choice of strokes kick	On :30
100	Free	Swim-down

3,037½   yards + ? × 50 yards total

WORKOUT 15

Distance	Stroke	Time
10:00	Free Alternate breathing Stroke Drill of your choice every 4th 25	Warm-up
25	Odd distances free	Rest :5 per 25 after
50	Even distances back	each distance
75		
100		
125		
150		
175		
200		
175		
150		
125		
100		
75		
50		
25		
4 × { 100 50 25	Back pull with buoy	Rest :10 after each distance
8 × 100	#1: 75 free, 25 back #2: 50 free, 50 back #3: 25 free, 75 back #4: 100 back #5: 25 back, 75 free #6: 50 back, 50 free #7: 75 back, 25 free #8: 100 free	On 1:40 (:15)
8 × 25	Back Very fast	On 1:00
200	Free	Swim-down
3,500 yards	+ 10:00 swim total	

The next five workouts are designed to help you build endurance in backstroke.

WORKOUT 16

Distance	Stroke	Time
400	Back	Warm-up
	25 right arm	
	25 left arm	
	25 Stroke Drill 28	
	25 normal	
	Repeat × 4	
500	Free: Easy	Rest :20 between
100	Back: Hard	swims
400	Free: Easy	
200	Back: Hard	
300	Free: Easy	
300	Back: Hard	
200	Free: Easy	
400	Back: Hard	
100	Free: Easy	
500	Back: Hard	
400	I.M.	
	Choice of strokes kick	
200	Free	Swim-down
4,000	yards total	

WORKOUT 17

Distance	Stroke	Time
200	Back	Warm-up
150	Breast	
100	Free	
50	Fly	
50	Back	Rest :10 per 50 after
100		each distance
150		
200		
200		
150		
100		
50		
25	Choice of strokes pull with buoy	Rest :5 per 25 after
50		each distance
75		
100		
100		
75		
50		
25		
800	Back	
	25 easy, 25 hard	
	50 easy, 50 hard	
	75 easy, 75 hard	
	100 easy, 100 hard	
	75 easy, 75 hard	
	50 easy, 50 hard	
	25 easy, 25 hard	
400	I.M. kick	Rest :20 after each
200		distance
100		
200	Back	For time
100	Free	Swim-down
3,800	yards total	

WORKOUT 18

Distance	Stroke	Time
400	I.M. reverse order 50 kick, 50 swim each stroke	Warm-up
250	Back	Rest :20 after each
200	Back	distance
3 × 100	I.M.	
200	Back	
150	Back	
2 × 100	I.M.	
150	Back	
100	Back	
100	I.M.	
400	Alternate 25 free, 25 back pull with buoy	
200	Back kick	Rest :10 after each
2 × 100		distance
4 × 50		
400	Alternate 25 free, 25 back	
200	Free	Swim-down
3,650	yards total	

WORKOUT 19

Distance	Stroke	Time
500	Alternate 50 free, 50 back	Warm-up
5 × 100	Back 25 kick, 25 right arm, 25 left arm, 25 normal	On 1:45 (:15)
100	Free	On 2:00
200	Times on the way down faster	On 3:00
300	than times on the way up	On 4:00
400		On 5:00
500		On 6:00
4 × 25	Easy	On :45
400		On 5:00
300		On 4:00
200		On 3:00
100		On 2:00
200	Choice of strokes	Swim-down
3,800	yards total	

WORKOUT 20

Distance	Stroke	Time
400	Alternate 25 free, 25 back, fists every 4th 25	Warm-up
4 × 100	Back pull with buoy	On 1:30 (:10)
4 × 300	#1: Alternate 25 back, 25 free #2: Alternate 50 back, 50 free #3: Alternate 75 back, 75 free #4: Alternate 100 back, 100 free	On 4:30 (:30)
6 × 125	Odd numbers alternate 25 back, 25 free Even numbers all back	On 1:45 (:15)
4 × 100	Back kick	On 2:00 (:10)
2 × 200	Back: For time #1: No break #2: Break :10 at 50s Beat #1 time by :10	Rest 2:00 between 200s
100	Free	Swim-down
3,650	yards total	

4
BREASTSTROKE

Several differences between the breaststroke and the other competitive strokes are immediately noticeable. First, you do the armstroke and the kick entirely underwater, which makes the breaststroke the slowest of all the strokes. Second, the arms and legs move more obviously like propellers, making full use of lift-dominated propulsion.

ARMSTROKE

The armstroke consists of an outsweep, a catch, a downsweep, an insweep, and a recovery. These motions flow together as one.

When you begin the armstroke, your arms are stretched fully forward in line with your body. Your hands then turn out at about a 45-degree angle and begin to travel outward with the elbows straight. Once the hands are approximately two feet apart (for adult swimmers), your elbows start to bend, and the stroke moves into the catch phase. Contrary to past breaststroke theory, your hands should travel wide apart before the elbows bend.

As the catch begins, the hands angle to a backward and outward pitch while the elbows bend into position for the most propulsive phase of the stroke, the downsweep.

During the downsweep, the arms, still bent at the elbows and led by the hands, sweep downward and outward in a circular path, creating a propeller motion. The speed of the hands increases through this phase.

The hands continue to accelerate into the insweep as they rotate from a downward and outward to a downward and inward pitch, and the hands begin moving toward one another and slightly upward.

The recovery begins as your hands come together under your chin. The pressure against the water is released at this point, and the hands turn palms down and streamline forward.

KICK

The currently used breaststroke kick employs a relatively narrow whiplike action with the feet acting like propellers. It consists of a recovery, an outsweep, a downsweep, an insweep, and a glide. These flow without interruption into a single motion.

The leg recovery begins just as your arms complete the insweep, because this is the point at which your hips are the lowest. Your knees drop downward and outward while your feet stay narrower than the knees. Your heels then travel forward and upward toward the buttocks as the knees flex. At the same time, the toes also flex toward the knees. It is precisely at these flexion points that well-developed ankle flexibility can lend tremendous propulsion.

Once your feet are slightly above your buttocks, and your knees are almost shoulder width apart, the feet whip outward and backward until the legs are almost extended. The soles of your feet should be facing backward and outward with the toes pointing out.

During the downsweep, the legs reach for full extension and begin sweeping downward as well as outward and backward. The toes are still turned up toward the knees and pointing out. The hips rise slightly at this point in the kick, causing a dolphinlike motion similar to the butterfly stroke, during which the body "falls" forward.

When the legs are fully extended, the insweep begins.

The outsweep

Sideview of the outsweep

The outsweep showing hips rising

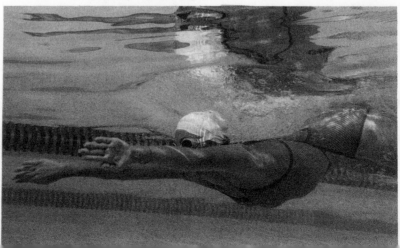

The beginning of the catch

The downsweep

The insweep

The recovery

The recovery as the propulsive phase of the kick begins

The toes rotate from pointing outward to pointing downward, truly like a propeller, and the feet change from moving downward to moving inward with the feet pitched inward. This motion lasts until the feet come nearly together and are on the same level as the hips.

A glide occurs after the insweep so that your legs will be in a streamlined position when the arm pull takes place.

BODY POSITION AND BREATHING

As in all of the competitive strokes, you should carry your hips close to the surface, and recovery should be as streamlined as possible. Your head must break the surface during at least some part of every stroke (with the exception of the underwater pullout described later).

To breathe, you lift your head and shoulders upward and forward during the downsweep of the arms. You inhale only while your head is lifted and exhale with your face in the water. The water surface should be at about the hairline. Breathing should take place during every stroke, because unlike in the other strokes, it assists rather than hinders proper timing.

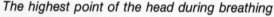

The highest point of the head during breathing

TIMING

Since recovery takes place underwater, streamlining is critical. For this reason, the legs must not begin their recovery until the arms are performing the insweep. Coordination should be fairly simple if you do this one aspect of timing properly. Unfortunately, less experienced swimmers tend to rush into the kick too soon.

UNDERWATER PULLOUT

In breaststroke races you are allowed one complete stroke underwater (without the head breaking the surface) following the start and each turn. Since the underwater pullout is more powerful than the surface armstroke, it can be a great advantage to you.

The underwater pullout starts with a glide after the dive or push-off from the wall. The body should be totally streamlined with arms extended, ears between your arms, legs extended and toes pointed.

Long arm pull of the breaststroke in an underwater pullout

Once you slow to race speed, with your head still down, take a complete outsweep, catch, and downsweep. In place of a normal insweep, continue the downsweep past chin level and bring your hands, rotated backward, slightly inward. Follow this with the upsweep, during which your hands sweep outward, backward, and then upward until the elbows are extended. The palms are finally turned inward to contribute to streamlining.

A second glide again takes place as you slow to race speed. Next, begin the arm recovery and kick simultaneously, giving great care to bringing your hands upward and forward close to the underside of your body. Bring your head up as your hands pass under your chin, and time the final extension of your arms to coincide with the outsweep of the kick.

Once you have completed the pullout, your head must break the surface before you begin your next armstroke.

QUICK CHECKLIST

Underwater Armstroke
1. Arms extend.
2. Hands turn out 45 degrees.
3. Hands go outward with elbows straight.
4. When hands are two feet apart, elbows bend.
5. Hands angle backward and outward.
6. Hands lead in, sweeping down and out.
7. Hand speed accelerates.
8. Hands rotate downward and inward.
9. Recovery begins with hands under chin.
10. Hands move forward to extension with palms down.

Kick
1. Recovery begins as arms complete insweep.
2. Knees drop downward and outward.
3. Feet stay close together.
4. Heels travel forward and upward.
5. Ankles flex.

6. Feet whip around when heels near buttocks.
7. Soles face backward and outward.
8. Toes point out.
9. Legs sweep downward, outward, and backward.
10. Hips rise.
11. Legs extend fully.
12. Toes rotate downward.
13. Feet move inward.
14. Glide.

Body Position and Breathing
1. Hips stay close to surface.
2. Recovery is streamlined.
3. Head breaks surface.
4. Head and shoulders come upward and forward during breathing.
5. Inhale as head is up.
6. Exhale as head is down.
7. Waterline is at hairline.
8. Breathe every stroke.

Timing
1. Legs recover as arms do insweep.

Underwater Pullout
1. Glide with body streamlined.
2. Head stays down.
3. Downsweep continues past chin level.
4. Hands move slightly inward.
5. Hands sweep outward, backward, and upward.
6. Elbows extend.
7. Palms turn inward.
8. Make a second glide.
9. Arm recovery and kick begin simultaneously.
10. Arms recover close to body.
11. Head comes up as hands pass chin.
12. Arms reach extension as legs do outsweep.

BREASTSTROKE MINICLINIC*

The swimmers I have coached always seem to hunger for stroke correction. Perhaps it's partly to avoid the routine of training, but a 20-minute practice on some stroke drills can provide a great stroke tune-up, even if you swim by yourself.

During the breaststroke kick, unlike the kicks used in all of the other competitive strokes, the feet move out to the side rather than up and down. This creates lift-dominated propulsion because the feet move like propellers. An efficient kick has the following characteristics:

- Feet travel in a plane that parallels the surface of the water until the downward thrust at the end of the kick.
- Toes turn up toward knees during the propulsive phase.
- Heels are just below the surface during recovery.
- Toes point outward during the whipping motion of the legs.
- Knees reach shoulder width during the propulsive phase.
- Hips rise slightly at the end of the kick.

The following six stroke drills can help you develop these characteristics.

Stroke Drill 32—Hold on to the gutter of the pool with one hand, and place the other hand flat against the wall below the surface. Extend your body near the surface and kick, concentrating on feeling the resistance of the water against your legs and feet. Be careful that your feet don't break the surface.

Stroke Drill 33—Kick with your arms at your sides. Touch your heels with your hands on each kick. Although this

---

*"Breaststroke Mini-Clinic" adapted with permission from *Swim* magazine, P.O. Box 45497, Los Angeles, CA 90045.

may be awkward, it will help you to develop an even kick and learn the proper timing of your breathing.

Stroke Drill 34—Kick with your arms extended in front of you and your face in the water (no kickboard). Try not to move your hands when you lift your head to breathe. During the propulsive phase of your kick, think about turning your toes up toward your knees while pointing them out.

Stroke Drill 35—For added conditioning, do Stroke Drill 34, keeping your head and shoulders up throughout the stroke.

Stroke Drill 36—Try vertical breaststroke kicking in deep water with your hands on top of your head. If your kick is strong, you will be able to keep your head up to breathe.

Stroke Drill 37—Kick on your back with your arms at your sides. From time to time, take a look at the width of your kick. Make sure your knees stay closer together than your shoulders.

Stroke Drill 38—If you tend to have a scissors motion in your kick, try kicking close to the wall so the bottom of your toes touch the wall with each kick. Experiment with the wall on one side and then on the other.

The armstroke, like the kick, differs from the movement of all the other strokes. In the breaststroke, the arms recover below instead of above the surface. An efficient pull should have these characteristics:

- Before you begin the pull, arms extend forward as far as possible.
- Hands pull wider than shoulder width before beginning propulsive phase.
- Hands pull back no farther than chin level.
- Pull and recovery are all one motion.
- Pull occurs as legs recover.
- Have the feeling of falling downhill as you extend into the stroke.

Stroke Drill 39—Pull while lying on your stomach on the pool deck with the gutter or edge of the pool directly below your shoulders, arms extended over the water. Your arms should touch the pool wall at the end of each pull.

Stroke Drill 40—Pull while standing on the bottom of the pool with one foot in front of the other. Watch that you pull back to chin level with the elbows just below the surface.

Stroke Drill 41—Swim, starting with only a small wrist scull and progressing to a larger pull. This progression may take a length or several lengths of the pool.

Stroke Drill 42—Swim with a car-size inner tube around your body under your armpits. This will force you to keep your pull entirely out in front of your body and to keep your elbows high. Also, the added drag will contribute to your overall conditioning.

Stroke Drill 43—Swim, taking two kicks for every arm-stroke. Get the feeling of stretching forward with your whole body during the second kick.

Stroke Drill 44—Swim, counting 1 to yourself at the completion of each armstroke and 2 as your hips rise at the completion of each kick. Try to develop a sense of coming over the crest of a hill and tumbling down the other side.

You may decide to do these stroke drills in sequence from beginning to end, or you may pick and choose based on your own particular goals, skill, and time availability. Either way, the drills are intended to help you recognize and then concentrate on the key characteristics mentioned.

WORKOUTS

The next five workouts are designed to help you develop speed in the breaststroke.

WORKOUT 21

Distance	Stroke	Time
400	75 free, 25 breast, 50 free, 50 breast, 25 free, 75 breast, 100 breast	Warm-up
4 × 150	50 Stroke Drill 43 50 Stroke Drill 44 50 normal	Rest :20 between swims
3 × { 100 100 100	Breast No breaks Break :10 at 50 Break :5 at 25s. Descend from sets #1 to #3	Rest :20 between swims, 1:00 between sets
2 × 350	Kick 25 easy, 25 hard, 25 easy, 50 hard, 25 easy, 75 hard, 25 easy, 100 hard	Rest 1:00 between 350s
2 × 350	Breast pull with buoy and paddles 25 easy, 25 hard, 25 easy, 50 hard, 25 easy, 75 hard, 25 easy, 100 hard	Rest 1:00 between 350s
10 × 25	Breast Very fast	On :45
100	Free	Swim-down
3,650	yards total	

WORKOUT 22

Distance	Stroke	Time
200	Choice of strokes kick	Warm-up
200	Choice of strokes pull	
200	Choice of strokes swim	
4 × 100	Breast 50 Stroke Drill 33 50 normal Accelerate speed on 2nd 50	Rest :15 between swims
8 × 100	#1: 75 free, 25 breast #2: 50 free, 50 breast #3: 25 free, 75 breast #4: 100 breast #5: 25 breast, 75 free #6: 50 breast, 50 free #7: 75 breast, 25 free #8: 100 breast	On 1:45 (:15)
8 × 50	Breast Descend #1–#4, #5–#8	On 1:00 (:15)
8 × 50	Breast Very fast	On 1:15 (:35)
6 × 100	Pull with buoy Odd numbers I.M. Even numbers free	Rest :15 between swims
8 × 50	Kick 2 × 25 fly, 25 back 2 × 25 back, 25 breast 2 × 25 breast, 25 free 2 × 25 free, 25 fly	On 1:00
4 × 25	Breast with dive Race pace of 50	On :45
100	Free	Swim-down
3,800	yards total	

WORKOUT 23

Distance	Stroke	Time
500	Free Breast every 4th 25	Warm-up
3 × 1:00	Kick Stroke Drill 36	
6 × 75	Breast 25 pull, 25 kick, 25 swim	Rest :15 between 75s
6 × 75	I.M. Work turns	On 1:20 (:20)
6 × { 75 50 25	Increase speed to 50 race pace as distance decreases	On 1:15 (:15) On 1:00 (:15) On :30
6 × 75	I.M. kick	On 1:30
6 × 50	Breast Around-the-walls	On 1:00 (:10)
6 × { 50 25 Dive + 12½	Increase speed to faster than 50 race pace as distance decreases	On 1:00 (:15) On :45 (:25) On :45
100	Choice of strokes	Swim-down

3,675 yards + 3:00 kicking total

▬ WORKOUT 24 ▬

Distance	Stroke	Time
200	Free swim	Warm-up
200	Free kick	
200	Free pull	
8 × 25	Breast Stroke Drill 35	On :45
400	I.M. Descend 1st–4th 25 of each stroke	

	Distance	Stroke			Time	
3 ×	200	Breast #1: On 3:10	#2: On 3:00	#3: On 2:50
	100	On 1:50	On 1:40	On 1:30
	50	On 1:10	On 1:00	On :50

4 × 100	Free pull with buoy, paddles, and tube Breathe only between flags (middle 15 yards of pool)	Rest: :20 between 100s

	Distance	Stroke			Time	
3 ×	100	Breast #1: On 1:40	#2: On 1:30	#3: On 1:20
	50	On 1:10	On 1:00	On :50
	25	On :35	On :30	On :25

	Distance	Stroke
3 ×	:45	Choice of strokes kick: Hard
	:15	Easy
	:30	Hard
	:15	Easy
	:15	Hard
	:15	Easy
	200	Free — Swim-down

3, 375 yards + 6:45 kicking total

WORKOUT 25

Distance	Stroke	Time
10:00	Choice of strokes pull, kick swim	Warm-up
5 × 100	Kick #1: 100 I.M. #2: 25 back, 25 breast, 25 free, 25 fly #3: 25 breast, 25 free, 25 fly, 25 back #4: 25 free, 25 fly, 25 back, 25 breast #5: 100 I.M.	Rest :20 between 100s
5 × 100	Breast #1: No breaks #2: Rest :10 at 50s #3: Same as #2 but faster #4: Rest :10 at 25s #5: Same as #4	Rest 1:00 between 100s
25 50 75 100 100 75 50 25	Choice of strokes pull with buoy and paddles	Rest :5 per 25 between swims
20 × 50	Choice of strokes Odd numbers moderate Concentrate on stroke Even numbers fast Do all same stroke	On 1:00 (:15)
10 × 25	Free 0–1 breath per 25	On :35
200	Free	Swim-down
2,950	yards + 10:00 swim total	

The next five workouts are designed to help you build endurance in breaststroke.

WORKOUT 26

Distance	Stroke	Time
300	Free swim	Warm-up
150	Free pull	
150	Free kick	
16 × 25	4 fly	On :30
	4 back	
	4 breast	
	4 free	
	Descend 1–4 each stroke	
2 × { 50	Fly	Rest :10 per 50 after
100	50 fly, 50 back	each distance
150	50 fly, 50 back, 50 breast	
200	I.M.	
150	50 fly, 50 back, 50 breast	
100	50 fly, 50 back	
50	Fly	
400	Pull with buoy, paddles, and tube	
	Alternate 50 free, 50 breast	
400	Kick	
	Alternate 50 free, 50 breast	
400	Free	
	25 breathe every 3 strokes	
	25 breathe every 5 strokes	
	25 breathe every 7 strokes	
	25 breathe every 9 strokes	
	Repeat × 4	
100	Free	Swim-down
3,900	yards total	

WORKOUT 27

Distance	Stroke			Time
400	Choice of strokes			Warm-up
	100 swim			
	100 pull			
	100 kick			
	100 swim			
3 × 〈 300	Breast #1: On 4:40	#2: On 4:30	#3: On 4:20	
200	On 3:10	On 3:00	On 2:50	
100	On 1:50	On 1:40	On 1:30	
100	Free pull with buoy, paddles,			Rest :15 per 100 after
200	and tube			each swim
300	Breast every 4th 25			
300	Free kick			
200	Breast every 4th 25			
100				
100	Free			
	Easy			
200	Breast			
	For time			
100	Free			Swim-down
3,800	yards total			

WORKOUT 28

Distance	Stroke	Time
600	75 choice of strokes, 25 free Repeat × 6	Warm-up
6 × 75	25 Stroke Drill 37 25 Stroke Drill 33 25 normal	Rest :15 between 75s
600	Free	Rest :15 per 100 after
100	I.M.	each swim
400	Free	
200	I.M.	
200	Free	
300	I.M.	
4 × 100	Breast pull with buoy, swim #1: 25 pull, 75 swim #2: 50 pull, 50 swim #3: 75 pull, 25 swim #4: 100 pull	Rest :10 between 100s
4 × 100	Breast kick, swim #1: 25 kick, 75 swim #2: 50 kick, 50 swim #3: 75 kick, 25 swim #4: 100 kick	Rest :10 between 100s
200	Free	Swim-down
3,850	yards total	

WORKOUT 29

Distance	Stroke	Time
8:00	Choice of strokes	Warm-up
8 × 50	Breast 　25 Stroke Drill 43 　25 normal	On 1:00 (:15)
400 2 × 200 4 × 100	Breast 　Increase speed as distance 　decreases	Rest :15 per 100 　between swims
100	Free 　Easy	
200 2 × 100 4 × 50	Breast 　Increase speed as distance 　decreases	Rest :20 per 50 　between swims
400	Free pull with buoy, paddles, and 　tube Breast every 4th 25	
4 × 100 4 × 50	Choice of strokes kick: Hard 　　　　　　　　　　　　Easy	Rest :10 between 　swims
100	Free	Swim-down
3,400	yards + 8:00 swim total	

73

WORKOUT 30

Distance	Stroke	Time
400	I.M. reverse order 50 kick, 50 swim each stroke	Warm-up

300
200
100
	Choice of strokes pull with buoy
	    and paddles
		Rest :20 between
		    swims

3 × 200 3 × 200 3 × 200	Breast	On 3:15 (:25) On 3:05 (:15) On 2:55 (:5)
100	Free Easy	

2 × 250	Choice of strokes kick
	    25 moderate
	    50 faster
	    75 faster
	    100 fastest
		Rest :30 between
		    200s

8 × 25	Breast
	    Odd numbers concentrate on
	        stroke
	    Even numbers fast
		On :30 (:10)

200	Free	Swim-down
3,800	yards total	

5
BUTTERFLY

The butterfly actually originated as a type of breaststroke with an over-the-water recovery, but the stroke has evolved and now bears more similarities to the freestyle. The butterfly is a strenuous stroke by comparison, because a greater portion of the body rises up out of the water at one time than in any other stroke. You might say the lift force is doing double duty in the butterfly.

As with the freestyle, the armstroke in the butterfly combines a propulsive phase that extends the entire reach of the arms both to the front and to the rear with an over-the-water recovery. The kick is also similar to the freestyle. The feet travel up and down as they kick, rather than sideways as in the breaststroke.

ARMSTROKE

The armstroke is made up of a hand entry, an outsweep, a catch, a downsweep, an insweep, an upsweep, and a recovery. These work together to create one continuous motion.

Your hands enter at points just outside the shoulders, with the palms pitched outward about 45 degrees and the elbows slightly bent. Following their entry, the hands immediately begin to move outward.

The outsweep

The catch and the beginning
of the downsweep

The insweep

The upsweep

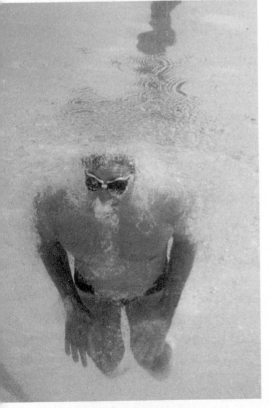

The catch

The downsweep

The insweep

The recovery

During the outsweep, your hands are pitched outward and backward and are actually driven forward as the elbows extend and the hips rise, forcing the shoulders downward and ahead. The hands then begin on a curved outward path, which puts them in good position for the catch.

The catch marks the beginning of the most propulsive phase of the armstroke and is aided by the last of the downward thrust from the kick. Here the pitch of the hands remains outward and backward, but also becomes slightly downward.

This downward pitch starts the hands on the downsweep, which is the continuation of the curved path begun during the outsweep.

The insweep begins, and your hands accelerate as your elbows start to bend. The hands sweep inward, upward, and backward under the body. The hands actually come very close to one another at the point of maximum elbow bend (approximately 90 degrees).

At this point, you have completed the curve begun with the outsweep, and the upsweep begins, forming a new curve sweeping outward, upward, and backward. The hands continue to accelerate throughout, and just before they leave the water to begin recovery, the palms turn inward so the hands slice out of the water, little fingers first.

During the recovery phase, your elbows are slightly flexed so they will leave the water just ahead of your hands. The hands then swing around with a wide lateral motion close to the surface.

KICK

The kicking motions in the butterfly, while similar to those in the freestyle, are performed with both legs moving together as a unit like a fishtail. The kick originates from the hips, so as to make maximum use of the whole leg. Therefore kneebend is minimal and present only on the downbeat. As the legs reach full extension on the downbeat, the hips rise and break the surface. The depth of the kick from the point at which the heels break the surface to full knee extension should be 12–16 inches.

As with the kicks for all of the strokes, good ankle flexibility is a key advantage. Turning your toes slightly inward on the downbeat will also allow you to deflect water off the tops of your feet more efficiently.

Most swimmers take two leg kicks for every arm cycle, but a few find that one comes more naturally. Two kicks, however, are preferable.

BODY POSITION AND BREATHING

For maximum efficiency in the butterfly, your body must bend in a loose, natural fashion, much like a flag waving in the wind. At the point of maximum bend in the stroke, the head is lower and the hips are higher than in any other stroke. This throws momentum ahead and helps you "fall" forward. But during the propulsive phase of the armstroke (the downsweep, the insweep, and the upsweep), the body is as near parallel to the surface as possible. Then, during arm recovery, the head and shoulders come completely up out of the water.

When your head submerges at the beginning of the underwater armstroke, your ears should be between your forearms, but your head should not be much below the surface, or excessive up-and-down motion is created. When your head comes up for a breath, the chin comes slightly forward so that it just clears the surface. If you can master the head position, you're in good shape, because your body will follow the motion of your head.

TIMING

For the body to bend in a loose, natural fashion, the downbeat of the first kick should come during the entry and the outsweep of the hands, and the upbeat should take place during the downsweep and the insweep of the arms. The downbeat of the second kick (which is missing if you use only one kick per armstroke) comes during the upsweep as the hands pass the hips, while the upbeat takes place during recovery.

Precision with the timing of the second kick is useful in

The body bend. Notice the high position of the hips and the lower position of the head, which cause forward momentum.

Butterfly breathing. Notice that the head and shoulders come completely out of the water at the start of the arm recovery.

three ways. First, it prevents the hands from pulling the hips too low during the propulsive phase of the armstroke. Second, it helps you push your hands out of the water at the end of the upsweep. Third, it raises the body so that lifting the head to breathe is easier.

Inhalation, with the chin just clearing the surface, occurs during the upsweep and the first portion of the recovery. In other words, the head reaches its highest point when the hips are at their lowest. The face then drops back into the water as the arms pass the shoulders. Notice that the head returns to its submerged position before the hands enter in front.

Horizontal body position, body bend, and rhythm are optimal when you do not breathe. Therefore the recommended breathing pattern is every other stroke. Some swimmers find this difficult, especially over distances, where oxygen demands are great. But realize that each lifting of the head detracts from body position, if only slightly.

With the diverse set of body positions required of an efficient butterfly stroke, overall precision in timing is critical to conserving energy and maintaining propulsion during this most strenuous of all the strokes. Practicing with swim fins can help provide balance and momentum for the novice who hasn't got everything just right yet, as well as for any swimmer who wants to increase ankle flexibility.

QUICK CHECKLIST
Underwater Armstroke
1. Hand entry is outside shoulders.
2. Palms are pitched 45 degrees.
3. Elbows are slightly bent.
4. Hands move outward, pitched outward and backward.
5. Shoulders move downward and ahead.
6. Hands curve in, pitched outward, backward, and downward.
7. Hands sweep down.
8. Hands sweep inward, upward, and backward.
9. Hands accelerate.
10. Elbows bend about 90 degrees.
11. Hands curve outward, upward, and backward.
12. Palms turn inward.
13. Hands slice out of the water.

Arm Recovery
1. Elbows flex slightly.
2. Hands leave water after elbows.
3. Hands swing around close to surface.

Kick
1. Kick originates from hips.
2. Knees bend slightly on downbeat.
3. Hips break the surface.
4. Depth of kick is 12–16 inches.
5. Toes turn in.
6. Kick twice for every arm cycle.

Body Position and Breathing
1. Body bends in loose, natural fashion.
2. Head submerges at hand entry.
3. Hips break the surface when head submerges.
4. Body parallels surface during arm propulsion.
5. Head and shoulders come up during recovery.
6. Ears are between forearms when head comes forward.
7. Chin comes forward when head comes up.

Timing
1. Downbeat of first kick is during hand entry and out-sweep.
2. Upbeat is during downsweep and insweep.
3. Downbeat of second kick is as hands pass hips.
4. Upbeat is during recovery.
5. Inhalation is during upsweep and beginning of recovery.
6. Face drops down as hands pass shoulders.
7. Best breathing pattern is every other stroke.

BUTTERFLY MINICLINIC*

What better way to improve your stroke than to go through a series of drills that will help you develop the feel for the water necessary for an efficient stroke? The following drills isolate particular characteristics of an effective kick, pull, and body position. You may do these drills in sequence for a complete stroke analysis, or you may pick and choose individual drills to spot check weak areas in your stroke or to add variety to your workout.

As you practice these next nine stroke drills, consider these characteristics of an effective kick.

- Kick from the hips down, not from the knees.
- Turn your toes in to improve propulsion.
- Be loose with your kick—like a flag waving in the wind.
- Emphasize downward motion of the feet, since this is the propulsive portion of the kick.

Stroke Drill 45—Stand with your feet together, six inches from the pool wall, your back toward the wall. Bounce your buttocks against the wall to create a dolphinlike action. This gives you a feel for using your hips to create the undulating motion of the kick.

Stroke Drill 46—Kick in place on the pool wall, one hand holding onto the gutter or the wall, the other flat against the wall about 18 inches below the surface. Concentrate on a slight knee bend on the downbeat of each kick and straight but not stiff knees on the upbeat.

Stroke Drill 47—Kick without a kickboard, your arms extended in front, your face in the water. Try to simulate the exact leg motions you practiced in Stroke Drill 46. If it feels different, go back to Stroke Drill 46, then repeat this drill.

Stroke Drill 48—Kick without a board, your arms at your

*"Butterfly Mini-Clinic" adapted with permission from *Swim* magazine, P.O. Box 45497, Los Angeles, CA 90045.

sides, your face in the water. Do not allow your shoulders to move up and down as you kick. This position will allow the easiest dolphin action and the greatest undulation.

Stroke Drill 49—Kick on your back, your arms at your sides. This drill will help to give you a feel for the propulsive part of the kick, which occurs when the legs extend.

Stroke Drill 50—Kick underwater with your arms either in front or at your sides. Once you have a sense of the kick with your feet completely submerged, you will have a better feel for your heels breaking the surface during the butterfly.

Stroke Drill 51—Kick on your side, one arm extended under your head, the other at your side. This drill will be referred to as "side kick." If you can do this drill, your coordination and feel for the kick are excellent.

Stroke Drill 52—Push off the wall, arms extended toward the bottom of the pool (preferably in shallow water). At the point where your hands touch the bottom, bring your feet down and push off the bottom toward the surface, thus creating a dolphinlike action. This drill will be referred to as "Porpoise" and will help you develop a smooth, undulating motion in your kick.

Stroke Drill 53—Kick with your arms extended in front. Do three kicks underwater, then three kicks on the surface. Repeat for the desired distance. This drill will help you coordinate your undulating motion with your kick.

Now that you have done some intensive work on improving your kick, here are some characteristics of an efficient pull to keep in mind as you practice the next five stroke drills:

- To promote long strokes, extend forward as far as possible at the beginning of your arm pull.
- To create momentum, push back hard at the end of each armstroke.

- Time your kicks so that one comes as your hands enter the water and the other as your arms leave the water at the end of each pull.
- Breathe as your shoulders come up to begin your arm recovery.

Stroke Drill 54—Kick six times with arms extended, then do one complete butterfly stroke (arms and legs). Repeat for the desired distance. This drill will help you coordinate the pull with the kick.

Stroke Drill 55—Swim three butterfly strokes on the surface, then duck your head and kick three times below the surface. Repeat for the desired distance. This drill will help you develop the dolphinlike action needed for proper body bend.

Stroke Drill 56—Swim butterfly using swim fins. The added propulsion from your kick (even if you haven't got it just right) will give you the freedom to work more closely on your pull, breathing, and timing.

Stroke Drill 57—Swim butterfly with one arm, the opposite arm extended in front. Breathe to the side. Repeat with the other arm. This exercise will help you with the timing of the kick, pull, and breathing.

Stroke Drill 58—Swim butterfly, taking one stroke with your right arm (left arm extended in front), then one stroke with the left arm (right arm extended in front), then one whole stroke. Repeat for the desired distance. This is yet another method to practice timing, and it's also a good coordination exercise.

Some careful work on the individual parts of the butterfly will be time well spent, since most swimmers agree that it is the most challenging of all the strokes. Swim fins are highly recommended for use with any drills on butterfly swimming because they will give you propulsion while forgiving any inefficiencies in your stroke. In addition, you'll be building ankle flexibility while having some fun.

WORKOUTS

The next five workouts are designed to help you develop speed in the butterfly.

━━━━━ WORKOUT 31 ━━━━━

Distance	Stroke	Time
200	Free: 25 free, 25 fly	Warm-up
	Repeat × 4	
200	Kick	
200	Free	
6 × 75	25 fly, 25 back, 25 breast	On 1:15 (:15)
	Emphasize speed on fly	
6 × 100	Free	On 1:40 (:20)
	Fly every 3rd 25	
100	Free	
	Easy	
6 × 100	Fly	On 1:20
	with fins	
6 × 50	25 fly, 25 free	On :55 (:15)
6 × 50	25 free, 25 fly	
12 × 50	Fly kick	On 1:00
4 × 25	Porpoise	On 1:00
100	Free	Swim-down

3,750   yards total

WORKOUT 32

Distance	Stroke	Time
300	Free	Warm-up
100	Stroke Drill 53	
100	Stroke Drill 55	
100	Free	
10 × 50	Fly kick 25 on right side 25 on left side	Rest :10 between 50s
100	Free Easy	
5 × 50	Breast	On :55 (:10)
5 × 50	Back	On :50 (:10)
5 × 50	Fly	On :45 (:5)
5 × 50	Free No extra rest when changing strokes	On :40 (:5)
10 × 50	Choice of strokes pull with buoy	On :55 (:15)
8 × 75	Fly 25 Stroke Drill 53 25 Stroke Drill 55 25 normal	Rest :5 before last 25 Rest :20 between 75s
100	Free Easy	
8 × 25	Odd numbers free easy Even numbers fly hard	On :30
100	Free	Swim-down
3,700	yards total	

WORKOUT 33

Distance	Stroke	Time
300	Free	Warm-up
300	Free, fly	
	Alternate 50 free, 50 Stroke Drill 58	
6 × 50	Pull with buoy	On :50 (:10)
	25 fly, 25 free	
6 × 50	25 free, 25 fly	
3 × 100	Free	On 1:40 (:20)
	1st 25 fly	
3 × 100	Free	
	2nd 25 fly	
3 × 100	Free	
	3rd 25 fly	
3 × 100	Free	
	4th 25 fly	
6 × 50	Kick	On :55
	25 fly, 25 free	
6 × 50	25 free, 25 fly	
12 × 50	Fly	On 1:15 (:30)
	#1–#3: Build speed	
	#4: Very fast	
	#5–#6: Build speed	
	#7–#8: Very fast	
	#9: Build speed	
	#10–#12: Very fast	
100	Free	Swim-down
3,700	yards total	

WORKOUT 34

Distance	Stroke	Time
300	I.M. reverse order	Warm-up
200	Choice of strokes kick	
100	Free	
4 × 150	Fly with fins 3rd 50 fastest	Rest :20 between swims
100	Free Easy	
4 × 100	Fly Descend Hold even pace during each 100	On 1:40 (:20)
2 × { 100 75 50 25	Choice of strokes pull with choice of equipment	Rest :10 per 50 after each swim
8 × 75	Fly 50 moderate, 25 fast	Rest :10 before last 25 Rest :20 between 75s
2 × { 100 75 50 25	Choice of strokes kick	Rest :10 per 50 after each swim
100	Free Easy	
12 × 12½	Fly Faster than best 25 divided by 2	On 1:00
100	Free	Swim-down
3,650	yards total	

WORKOUT 35

Distance	Stroke	Time
250	Choice of strokes pull with buoy	Warm-up
2 × 125	Fly kick	
	25 Stroke Drill 48	
	25 Stroke Drill 49	
	25 Stroke Drill 50	
	25 side kick on right side	
	25 side kick on left side	
250	Choice of strokes	
5 × 100	Fly	On 1:45 (:30)
	2nd 50 faster	
2 × 250	Choice of strokes pull with buoy, paddles, and tube	Rest :20 between 250s
10 × 50	Fly	On 1:00 (:20)
	2nd 25 fast	
4 × 125	Kick	Rest :10 between 125s
	#1 and #3: same as warm-up	
	#2 and #4: 50 fly, 25 back, 25 breast, 25 free	
20 × 25	Free	On :30
	Odd numbers moderate	
	Even numbers no breath	
100	Free	Swim-down
3,350	yards total	

The next five workouts are designed to help you develop endurance in the butterfly.

WORKOUT 36

Distance	Stroke	Time
600	Alternate 50 free, 50 choice of strokes	Warm-up
100	Pull with buoy, 1st 25 fly	Rest :15 between swims
100	Free, 2nd 25 fly	
100	Free, 3rd 25 fly	
100	Free, 4th 25 fly	
2 × { 200	Free, 1st 25 fly	Rest :30 between swims
200	Free, 2nd 25 fly	
200	Free, 3rd 25 fly	
200	Free, 4th 25 fly	
100	Free, 1st 25 fly	Rest :15 between swims
100	Free, 2nd 25 fly	
100	Free, 3rd 25 fly	
100	Free, 4th 25 fly	
100	Free Easy	
2 × 200	Fly #1: Rest :20 at 100 #2: Rest :10 at 50s	Rest 2:00 between 200s
200	Free	Swim-down
3,700	yards total	

WORKOUT 37

Distance	Stroke	Time
100	Free	Warm-up
100	Breast	
100	Back	
100	Fly	
100	Free	
4 × { 2:00	Choice of strokes: Hard	
1:00	Easy	
500	Alternate 25 fly, 25 free	Rest :30 between
400	Free	swims
300	Alternate 25 fly, 25 free	
200	Free	
100	Alternate 25 fly, 25 free	
500	I.M. pull with buoy	
	400 I.M. + 100 fly	
4 × 125	I.M.	On 1:50 (:20)
	50 fly, 25 back, 25 breast, 25 free	
200	Free	Swim-down
3,200	yards + 12:00 kick total	

WORKOUT 38

Distance	Stroke	Time
500	Free with alternate breathing	Warm-up
8 × 50	2 × 25 fly, 25 back 2 × 25 back, 25 breast 2 × 25 breast, 25 free 2 × 25 free, 25 fly	On :55 (:15)
5 × 200	#1: 200 I.M. #2: 50 back, 50 breast, 50 free, 50 fly #3: 50 breast, 50 free, 50 fly, 50 back #4: 50 free, 50 fly, 50 back, 50 breast #5: 200 I.M.	On 3:15 (:30)
100	Free Easy	
5 × 100	Fly pull with buoy	On 1:45 (:20)
5 × 100	Fly Descend	On 1:45 (:25)
8 × 50	Kick 2 × 25 fly, 25 back 2 × 25 back, 25 breast 2 × 25 breast, 25 free 2 × 25 free, 25 fly	On 1:00
4 × 25	Porpoise	On 1:00
200	Free	Swim-down
3,700	yards total	

WORKOUT 39

Distance	Stroke	Time
200	Free	Warm-up
150	Your weakest stroke	
100	Your specialty	
50	Free	
500	Alternate 25 fly, 25 free	
5 × 100	Free	On 1:40 (:20)
	#1: Breathe every 3 strokes	
	#2: Breathe every 4 strokes	
	#3: Breathe every 5 strokes	
	#4: Breathe every 6 strokes	
	#5: Breathe every 7 strokes	
5 × 200	Fly	Rest :45 between
	Even pace	200s
100	Free	
	Easy	
300	I.M.	Rest :20 between
3 × 100	Fly kick	swims
4 × 75	Pull with buoy	
	25 fly, 25 back, 25 breast	
200	Free	Swim-down
3,700	yards total	

WORKOUT 40

Distance	Stroke	Time
100	Choice of strokes: Swim	Warm-up
100	Pull	
100	Kick	
100	Swim	
400	I.M. broken	Rest :10 at 25s
	Descend 1st–4th 25 of each stroke	
6 × 250	I.M.	On 4:00 (:40)
	100 fly, 50 back, 50 breast, 50 free	
400	Choice of strokes pull with choice of	Rest :10 per 100
200	equipment	between strokes
100		
3 × 200	Kick	Rest :30 between
	#1: Alternate 50 fly, 50 back	200s
	#2: Alternate 50 fly, 50 breast	
	#3: Alternate 50 fly, 50 free	
200	Fly	
	For time	
100	Free	Swim-down
3,900	yards total	

6
STARTS AND TURNS

Sometimes the importance of what a swimmer does on the walls takes a back seat to what he or she does between the walls. This is understandable considering the value of training time and the great many skills you must develop. Starts and turns do, however, play a critical role in the overall efficiency of a race. Often, particularly in the sprint events, the difference between first place and sixth place may be less than two seconds. Where it might take you months to shave a second or more off your swimming time, improving your starts and turns might do it in a few weeks.

Starts are of two types: out of the water and in the water. An out-of-the-water start is used for freestyle, breaststroke, and butterfly, while an in-the-water start is used for backstroke. When doing any kind of start, the object is to get off the starting block quickly and to enter the water, arms first, in as streamlined a position as possible.

Turns, too, are of two types: flip turns and open turns. Flip turns are the fastest and are used in freestyle and backstroke. In the breaststroke and butterfly, which require a two-hand wall touch, an open turn is used.

THE PIKE START

The pike start is the name given to the newest start, which is considered the most efficient out-of-the-water start. The best reason to learn this dive is speed, but a close

96

second is that it looks so graceful and is highly impressive.

In the old days, I was taught that the best way to begin a race was to fling myself headlong out over the water and land as flat as possible on the surface so as to prevent downward movement into the water. More recently, experts have discovered that this practice not only stops downward movement, but curbs momentum as well. Imagine, for example, the difficulty of pounding a nail into a board with its flat head first as compared to the ease of putting it in point first. In this concept lies the key to the increased efficiency of the pike start.

An efficient start is one in which your body comes into contact with as small an area of the water as possible, while still allowing you a sufficiently shallow entry to surface easily. This permits you to travel the greatest distance from the starting block before you begin swimming. However, more of this distance is underwater than with the old flat dive.

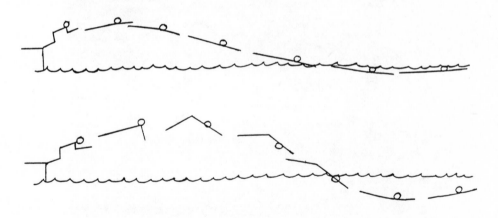

Notice in the figures that the angle of entry into the water is much sharper with the pike dive than the flat dive. This allows you to slip through the surface with minimal resistance and thereby travel a considerable distance at high speed below the surface.

To create this angle, use the following sequence. **Practice with extreme caution and only in water at least six feet deep until you are proficient. Do not dive into shallow water.**

Bend over and grab the front of the starting block with your hands as you flex your knees. Your weight should be forward. Let your head drop low so that you are looking between your legs at the back of the starting block.

As you take off, lift your head high enough to get a look at the opposite end of the pool or the backstroke flags.* This is the key to getting the height you need for a proper pike dive. Realize that the motion of your body will follow the motion of your head, so if you want your body to go higher, lift your head. If you want your body to go lower, drop your head. But in any case, be sure to lift your head as soon as your body enters the water, so you stop your downward movement.

*See Glossary.

98

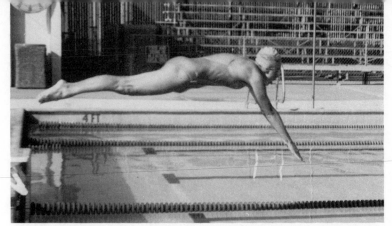

By stopping the forward motion of your arms when they are directly below your shoulders, you are in position to angle your body down sharply once you reach the full height of your dive.

To begin your downward angle, drop your head into the space between your arms and allow your body to bend or pike at the waist. Also, streamline your body by pointing your toes and squeezing your ears between your arms.

To stop your downward motion, lift your head to an ears-between-your-arms position once your body enters the water.

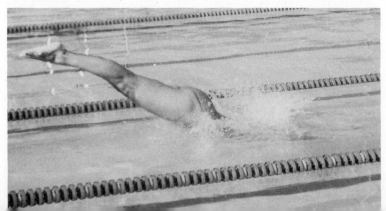

The following drills are designed to help you develop and practice the skills necessary for an efficient pike dive. You can do all of them from the side of the pool as well as the starting block. Starting from the side may be used as a preliminary step to reduce anxiety.

Start Drill 1—Place a hula hoop on the surface of the water about six to eight feet from the end of the pool below your starting block. Practice jumping off the starting block through the hoop.

Start Drill 2—Begin in a normal bent-over starting position on the block. Then swing your arms forward to the correct position as you begin to take off, but instead of going in the water head first, bring your legs forward to touch your hands, and enter feet first.

Start Drill 3—Repeat Start Drill 2, using a hula hoop as described in Start Drill 1.

Start Drill 4—Practice diving through a hula hoop 6–8 feet in front of the starting block.

Start Drill 5—Dive with your toes about a foot from the front edge of the starting block rather than with your toes over the edge.

Start Drill 6—Have someone hold a long pole at least six inches higher than the level of the starting block and at least a foot and a half in front of it. Practice diving over the pole. It can be raised and moved farther out as your skill increases. (Tapping the pole with your feet does not hurt.)

With practice on these drills and the desire to soar like an eagle, you'll surely go far, especially from the starting block.

QUICK CHECKLIST
1. Grab the starting block as knees flex.
2. Pitch weight forward.

3. Lift head high.
4. Stop forward motion of arms below shoulders.
5. Drop head between arms.
6. Bend at waist.
7. Point toes.
8. Squeeze ears between arms.
9. Lift head as soon as body enters water.

THE BACKSTROKE START

The conventional backstroke start begins and ends in the water, although a starting block is still used because it provides a backstroke start rail reachable from in the water. This rail allows you to pull yourself up into a more advantageous position for the backward thrust than merely using the side of the pool.

When doing an in-the-water start, coming into contact with as small an area of the water as possible is as critical as with an out-of-the-water start. Therefore, the backstroke start is done with a sharper angle of entry than it was some years ago, just as the pike start has replaced the old flat dive. To create that angle, follow this sequence:

1. Grip the backstroke start rail with hands about shoulder width apart. Place your toes and balls of your feet on top of the gutter or against the wall. (Placing them on top of the gutter will give you more leverage.)
2. Pull yourself up out of the water in a crouched position. Your head should be down.
3. Drive upward and backward with your legs as you throw your head way back and bring your arms, slightly flexed, around behind your head. You should catch a glimpse of the other end of the pool as your toes leave the wall.
4. The motion of your head will cause your body to travel through the air in an arc clearing the water completely. This height will eliminate any drag on the

101

water during the propulsive phase of the start and will position you for a good clean entry.

5. Enter the water in streamlined position as if through a hole. Your ears should be between your arms, and your toes pointed.

6. To stop your downward motion following the entry, bring your chin down.

Start Drill 7—Lay a kickboard on the surface about three feet from the end of the pool. Practice backstroke starting over the board without touching it.

QUICK CHECKLIST

1. Grip start rail, hands at shoulder width.
2. Place toes and balls of feet on gutter.
3. Drive upward and backward with legs.
4. Throw head way back.
5. Bring arms around slightly flexed.
6. Body clears surface.
7. Keep ears between arms.
8. Point toes.
9. Entry is streamlined.
10. Bring chin down.

THE FREESTYLE FLIP TURN

The freestyle flip turn closely resembles a front somersault, with the addition of a last-moment twist that brings the swimmer onto his or her stomach. The technique is one worth perfecting when you consider that each turn, including the push-off, takes more than two seconds. Besides, a flip turn looks as impressive as a pike dive.

There is no question that a flip turn is a fast way to turn around, and becoming faster. In my early days of swimming, we had to touch the wall with a hand in addition to the feet, but this has since been dropped. Also, the practice of pushing off the wall so that the side of the body rather than the stomach faces the bottom of the pool has, in the interest of speed, become popular.

Practicing the following sequence will help you perfect an efficient freestyle flip turn:

1. Begin planning for your turn four to five strokes from the wall so that you will be a suitable distance from the wall when you need to turn.
2. The last stroke before the turn, keep one arm at your side while the other arm pulls down hard, your chin tucks down, and your body follows the pulling arm around, making a somersaulting motion.
3. As your legs come out of the water and pass over your head, tuck your knees so that your feet stay close to the surface and you flip over more quickly.
4. As your feet approach the wall, turn your head slightly away from the side of your pulling arm, and begin extending your arms and body for the push-off just before your feet make contact with the wall.
5. Place your feet on the wall at a 45-degree angle toward the side you're facing. Your knees should be flexed for the push-off.
6. As you push away from the wall, gradually rotate from a position where your side faces the bottom of the pool to one where you're on your stomach. Be sure to streamline your glide by keeping your ears between your arms and pointing your toes. Also, make certain that your body is completely submerged throughout the push-off.

Doing the following drills in sequence will provide you with a step-by-step method of learning the freestyle flip turn.

Turn Drill 1—Making use of waist- to chest-deep water, begin by standing, feet together, and bringing your upper body down into a tuck position. Then, using your arms to

The tuck

After the flip, your feet should be at a 45-degree angle and touching the wall. Legs should be flexed for the push-off.

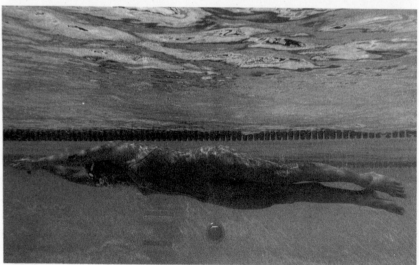

Streamline the push-off glide by keeping your ears between your arms and pointing your toes.

push yourself around, do a full somersault and return to a standing position, facing the same direction as when you began. You'll discover that you must keep your eyes open to do this.

Turn Drill 2—Same as Turn Drill 1, except you begin from a swimming position rather than a standing position, so that you complete three-quarters of a somersault.

Turn Drill 3—Swim up to the wall and complete a half-somersault, placing your feet on the wall, toes up, and pushing off on your back.

Turn Drill 4—Same as Turn Drill 3, except your feet touch the wall at a 45-degree angle and you push off on your side rather than on your back.

QUICK CHECKLIST

1. Plan turn four to five strokes out from wall.
2. Keep one hand at side, while the other hand pulls down hard.
3. Do a chin tuck.
4. Body follows hand into somersault.
5. Legs come over body in tuck position.
6. Head turns as feet approach wall.
7. Arms and body extend for push-off before feet touch wall.
8. Feet touch wall at 45-degree angle, knees flexed.
9. Rotate from side to stomach as you push off.
10. Keep ears between arms.
11. Point toes.
12. Body is submerged throughout push-off.

THE BACKSTROKE FLIP TURN

The backstroke flip turn comes in several varieties, including the spin turn, the Naber turn, and—the newest—

the roll turn. There are at least as many schools of thought as to which one is fastest. The Naber turn and the roll turn are more difficult to learn and have some distinct disadvantages if you perform them incorrectly. Therefore, this discussion will concern only the spin turn. If you are interested in the others, refer to Ernest Maglischo's book *Swimming Faster.*

The backstroke flip turn is in several ways easier to learn than the freestyle flip turn. However, it sometimes causes greater anxiety because you go into the wall without being able to see it. The good news is that, since your back remains parallel to the surface throughout, you are less likely to become disoriented than during the somersaulting of the freestyle turn. The turn really is more of a spin turn, in which your head and hips switch positions, than a flip turn as in the freestyle. Perhaps the greatest advantage to learning the backstroke turn is that you can perform it entirely, including push-off, on land.

Practicing the following sequence will help you develop an efficient backstroke flip turn:

1. Learn to watch for the backstroke flags, and count the number of strokes it takes you to swim from them to the end of the pool. If flags are not available where you swim, you can count the number of strokes you take for each entire length (which takes a lot of concentration), or you can watch for other landmarks or features of the pool.

2. If you must look back, turn your head to the side as the arm on that side enters the water, so as to cause as little disruption to your stroke as possible.

3. As one arm stretches back to meet the wall, bring your head back so you are looking underwater at the point on the wall where your hand will touch.

4. Place your hand on the wall, fingers pointing down, with your elbow slightly flexed.

5. With your contact hand, push upward and backward against the wall for leverage as your legs come out of

109

As your arm stretches back to meet the wall, your head should be tilted back, so that you can look at the point of the wall where your hand will make contact.

With your contact hand, push upward and backward as your legs swing out of the water, knees flexed.

the water, knees flexed. Remove your hand only to make way for your legs, which will come around above the surface on the same side, as your head and hips switch positions.

6. As your feet, toes pointing upward, touch the wall where your hand was, your arms are already stretching back over your head for the push-off. At this point, your knees are still flexed.

7. Push off in a streamlined position with your ears between your arms and your toes pointed. Make sure your body is completely submerged throughout the push-off.

8. Once your push-off speed begins decreasing, do a powerful butterfly kick before surfacing.

Turn Drill 5—To practice the backstroke flip turn on land, find a slippery floor such as one made of linoleum, and a scatter rug that will slide easily if turned nap down. Remove your shoes and lie down with the rug under your back. Extend your arm behind your head, keeping your elbow slightly flexed, and adjust your position on the floor so that you can place your palm with fingers pointing down, against the wall.

From this position, you will be able to bring your legs up and around, spin, place your feet on the wall, and push off. If space does not permit a push-off, or a slippery surface is unavailable, you can still practice the other movements.

QUICK CHECKLIST
1. Watch for backstroke flags.
2. Turn head to side to look when arm is back.
3. Bring head back as arm reaches for wall.
4. Fingers point down on wall touch.
5. Elbow is slightly flexed.
6. Push backward with contact hand as legs come around.
7. Knees are flexed.

8. Remove hand as feet come near wall.

9. Head and hips switch positions.

10. Arms stretch back.

11. Toes point upward as feet touch wall.

12. Knees remain flexed.

13. Streamline as you push off.

14. Ears go between arms.

15. Toes are pointed.

16. Body is submerged during push off.

17. Use a butterfly kick before surfacing.

THE BREASTSTROKE AND BUTTERFLY TURN

Because a flip turn is not practical when both hands must touch the wall simultaneously before turning, an open turn is used with the breaststroke and butterfly. The only difference between the breaststroke and the butterfly turns is that the push-off of the breaststroke is slightly deeper to accommodate the long underwater pullout described in Chapter 4.

An efficient breaststroke or butterfly turn uses the following sequence of movements:

1. Plan your distance to the wall two to three strokes out, so that you do not get caught short or long.
2. Stretch for the wall so that both hands make contact simultaneously.
3. As you touch the wall, your knees are already bending and are beginning to come in to the wall in preparation for the turnaround.
4. One hand quickly drops from the wall: then the same shoulder drops as the hand begins to stretch backward for the push-off. The legs are now tucked tightly.
5. The second hand begins to swing around above the surface to join the first, just before your feet touch the wall.

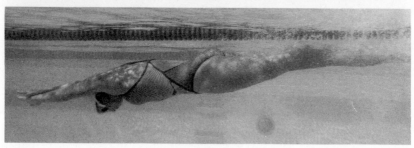

The open turn

6. Grab a quick breath of air before your hands meet in front and you bring your head down between your ears for the push-off.

7. Push off in a streamlined position with your toes pointed, making sure your body is submerged throughout.

QUICK CHECKLIST

1. Anticipate wall.
2. Stretch for wall with two hands.
3. Touch wall as knees are bending.
4. Hand and shoulder drop.
5. Hand stretches back.
6. Legs are tucked.
7. Second hand swings forward.
8. Feet touch wall.
9. Take a quick breath.
10. Head drops; ears go between arms.
11. Hands meet in front.
12. Push off in streamlined position.
13. Point toes.
14. Body is submerged during push-off.

7
TRAINING PHASES

Once you've been swimming for some time and find you
are interested in competition, you're going to face the challenge of organizing your workouts so as to prepare yourself
for goals that take longer than a week or two to achieve. If
you have a coach, you'll have some help in this area. But
you alone must make the decision to invest time and effort
in raising your swimming ability to levels possible only
through a long-range plan.

This approach is truly an investment because in following the training phases of a swimming season, you will be
exchanging short-term success for long-term victory. You
will be intensifying your training. Temporarily your swimming times may be slower, but at the points you decide on
ahead of time, they'll be faster.

The first step is to divide your swimming season into
three phases: early season, midseason, and taper. If you follow these phases in sequence and for the proper length of
time, they will help you achieve a physiological (and to
some degree psychological) peak immediately after the
taper period.

Your swimming season should be up to six months long.
Typically a year includes a short-course season, in which
competition takes place in a 25-yard pool, and a long-

115

course season, in which competition takes place in a 50-meter pool. Ideally, early season training would account for about eight weeks, midseason six to eight weeks, and taper about three weeks. However, the exact amount of time you spend on each phase depends on how you respond to different kinds of training.

Following a phased program may mean that during the early and intermediate stages of the season, your times are not as fast as you'd like them to be. But be farsighted enough to realize that you must first wear yourself down in order to build yourself up to a higher level of ability. You'll be surprised at how quickly your times will drop with a little rest after the hard work.

EARLY SEASON TRAINING

The purpose of early season training is to lay the groundwork for the more strenuous phase of training to follow, much as base training lays the foundation for specificity training. A solid base of good stroke mechanics, for example, is necessary if you are to avoid strain or injuries during midseason training. This is the stage in which to begin any land exercises for strength and flexibility (see Chapter 8). You should also do distance swimming well within your capacity to develop good circulatory efficiency. Interspersed with this distance work should be a few shorter swims at higher heart rates to begin building a base for speed.

In other words, the early season phase is about 90 percent base training. The swims are frequently of odd distances, such as 750 yards or 225 yards, to discourage any concern with times. For the same reason, during interval swimming a fixed amount of rest is used more often than a fixed send-off time.

Also, spend some time doing drills such as one-arm swimming or isolating other parts of the stroke to improve strength and balance. Attention to starts and turns for all strokes, constantly analyzing the efficiency of your movements, is a good practice as well. Resistance devices, such as hand paddles, tubes, extra bathing suits, T-shirts, or anything that will add variety while building strength and endurance, are of primary importance during the early season. Kicking and pulling are also excellent. Even a nonswimming exercise that contributes significantly to cardiovascular fitness might take the place of a little of your distance swimming during this phase.

The following workouts are typical of those appropriate for the early season.

WORKOUT 41

Distance	Stroke	Time
200	Choice of strokes swim	Warm-up
200	Choice of strokes kick	
200	Choice of strokes pull	
2 × { 100	Alternate 25 fly, 25 free	Rest :15 per 100 after
100	Alternate 25 back, 25 free	each swim
100	Alternate 25 breast, 25 free	
300	Free	
200	I.M.	
2 × { 100	Free pull with buoy, paddles, and	Rest :10 after each
200	tube	distance
2 × { 200	Free kick	Rest :10 after each
100		distance
5:00	Practice dives	
100	Free	Swim-down

3,500   yards + 5:00 dive practice total

WORKOUT 42

Distance	Stroke	Time
500	Free with alternate breathing	Warm-up
2 × 225	Back 25 right arm 25 left arm 25 normal Repeat × 2	Rest :30 between 225s
500	Back kick with fins, arms extended behind head Do each 50 a different stroke than the preceding 50	
2 × 225	Breast 25 Stroke Drill 37 25 Stroke Drill 43 25 normal	Rest :30 between 225s
500	Fly with fins	Rest :10 at 100s
500	Free pull with buoy, paddles, and tube, and wearing T-shirt or shorts over suit	
100	Free	Swim-down
3,000	yards total	

━━ **WORKOUT 43** ━━

Distance	Stroke	Time
400	Free with alternate breathing	Warm-up

8:00	Free
	    Count strokes every 4th 25
	    Make sure count stays even	

8:00	100 I.M.s continuous	
8:00	Your specialty kick	Rest :10 at each 50

8:00	Free
	    25 Breathe every 3 strokes
	    25 Breathe every 5 strokes
	    25 Breathe every 7 strokes
	    25 Breathe every 9 strokes	

300
200
100
	Choice of strokes pull with choice
	    of equipment
		Rest :20 between
		    swims

100	Free	Swim-down

1,110   yards + 24:00 swim + 8:00 kick total

WORKOUT 44

Distance	Stroke	Time
4 × 100	Free 25 right arm, 25 left arm, 25 catch-up, 25 ripple	Warm-up
Up to 50	Press-ups* Spend no more than 5:00	
1,000	Free Your specialty every 4th 25	
4 × 100	Free 50 baton, 50 normal	Rest :20 between 100s
4 × 125	Choice of strokes pull with buoy Around-the-walls	Rest :20 between 100s
500	400 I.M. + 100 fly	
4 × 125	Kick (no board) #1: 50 fly, 25 back, 25 breast, 25 free #2: 25 fly, 50 back, 25 breast, 25 free #3: 25 fly, 25 back, 50 breast, 25 free #4: 25 fly, 25 back, 25 breast, 50 free	Rest :20 between 125s
100	Free	Swim-down

3,400   yards + up to 50 press-ups total

*See Chapter 8.

WORKOUT 45

Distance	Stroke	Time
400	I.M. reverse order of strokes 50 kick, 50 swim of each stroke	Warm-up
50	Free	Rest :15 per 50 at the
100	I.M.	end of each
150	Free	distance
200	I.M.	
250	Free	
250	Free	
200	I.M.	
150	Free	
100	I.M.	
50	Free	
500	Free pull with buoy, paddles, and tube	

4 × 250	#1: 1st and 10th 25 fly
	#2: 1st and 10th 25 back
	#3: 1st and 10th 25 breast
	#4: 1st and 10th 25 your weakest
	    stroke
		Rest :30 between
		    250s

500	Kick 400 I.M. + your weakest stroke	
5:00	Practice turns	
100	Free	Swim-down
3, 500	yards + 5:00 turn practice total	

MIDSEASON TRAINING

Midseason training is the most strenuous workout phase and is probably equal to or slightly shorter in weeks than early season training. The hazard with midseason training, because of the intensity of the workouts, is overtraining. Some swimmers will be able to tolerate more work without failing to adapt to the stress of training. For this reason, the percentages of base training versus specificity training will vary. In general, the midseason phase consists of 75–80 percent specificity training and only 20–25 percent base training. However, if you grow fatigued and lose your enthusiasm for swimming, some rest might be a good prescription. Tipping the scale slightly toward the base training side for a time also may help.

Characteristic of midseason training, as compared with earlier training is more repeat swims in a set, more fixed send-off intervals, and slightly longer rests between swims. This means that heart rate will go higher and race conditions will be more nearly simulated. You continue to work on starts and turns and on stroke techniques, but to a lesser degree because this phase places so many demands on time, and alterations in stroke technique take some time to become effective. You don't want to be caught in this adjustment period as you approach your taper.

Stroke specialization also plays an important role. You'll want to think about which strokes and events are most important to you and plan your training accordingly. Clearly if you're interested in emphasizing sprint events, you'll want to do more short-distance, high-intensity swimming and fewer long swims than if you want to specialize in distance events, and vice versa. Swimmers wishing to excel in one or more 200-yard distances would do well to divide their training between the two extremes. Sprinters do, however, need some distance swimming, because certain adaptations take place only at slower speeds and longer distances. For a converse reason, distance swimmers need some speed work.

Above all, your training should be closer to the maximum amount you can handle without excessive fatigue than at any other phase of training. You can accomplish this in a variety of ways, including doing negative split swims to promote even race pace, limiting breathing to increase lung capacity, and doing broken swims to simulate race pace.

Again, don't be discouraged if your times are off. Swimming fast and efficiently when tired is a skill you'll get better at.

The following workouts are typical for midseason.

━━━━━━━━━━━━━━━ **WORKOUT 46** ━━━━━━━━━━━━━━━

Distance	Stroke	Time
400	Free with alternate breathing 2nd 200 faster	Warm-up
3 × 150	Free Increase speed on each 50	On 2:15 (:30)
33 × 50	Free Get total swim time for 1,650 yards (subtract 5:20 rest time from total)	Rest :10 after each 50
100	Free Easy	
5 × 100	Your specialty pull with buoy and paddles Hold even times	On 1:40 (:2)
10 × 50	Kick Odd numbers free Even numbers your specialty	On 1:00
5:00	Practice breast turns	
100	Free	Swim-down
3,700	yards + 5:00 turns total	

━ WORKOUT 47 ━

Distance		Stroke	Time
	200	Free	Warm-up
	150	Your weakest stroke	
	100	Your specialty	
	50	Free	
2 ×	{ 200	Free: Get time	On 3:00 (:30)
	2 × 200	½ 200 time − :10	On 1:30 (:20)
	4 × 50	½ 100 time − :5	On :45 (:10)
	50	Free	
		Easy	
	100	Choice of strokes kick	Rest :10 between
	2 × 50	Increase speed as distance	kicks
	4 × 25	decreases	
2 ×	{ 200	Your specialty (no free): Get time	On 3:10 (:30)
	2 × 100	½ 200 time − :10	On 1:40 (:20)
	4 × 50	½ 50 time − :5	On :50 (:10)
	50	Free	
		Easy	
	100	Choice of strokes pull with buoy and	Rest :10 between
	2 × 50	paddles	pulls
	4 × 25	Increase speed as distance	
		decreases	
	100	Free	Swim-down

3,700   yards total

WORKOUT 48

Distance	Stroke	Time
100	Free swim	Warm-up
200	Free pull with buoy	
200	Free kick	
100	Free swim	
20 × 25	Choice of strokes pull with buoy Practice fast turnover	On :30
4 × 200	Free broken #1: 100/100 #2: 100/50/50 #3: 100/50/25/25 #4: 100/25/25/25/25	All breaks :10 Rest 1:00 between 200s
100	Free Easy	
4 × 200	Choice of strokes broken (all 1 stroke, no free) #1: 100/100 #2: 100/50/50 #3: 100/50/25/25 #4: 100/25/25/25/25	All breaks :10 Rest 1:00 between 200s
20 × 25	Kick 5 each stroke	On :30
10:00	Practice back start and dives	
100	Free	Swim-down
3,400	yards + 10:00 starts total	

WORKOUT 49

Distance	Stroke	Time
100	Right arm	Warm-up
100	Left arm	
200	Baton	
200	Normal	
16 × 100 + 50	Free	Rest :10 after each
	Get total swim time for 1,650 yards	100
	(subtract 2:40 rest time from total)	
100	Free	
	Easy	
6 × 75	Back	On 1:30 (:10)
	25 kick with arms behind head	
	25 right arm	
	25 left arm	
6 × 75	Back	On 1:20 (:10)
	Descend #1–#3, #4–#6	
2 × 200	Free pull with buoy, paddles, and	Rest :20 between
	tube	200s
	Descend	
100	Free	Swim-down
3,750	yards total	

WORKOUT 50

Distance	Stroke	Time
200	Free	Warm-up
150	Breast	
100	Back	
50	Fly	
12 × 75	3 × 50 fly, 25 back	On 1:30 (:20)
	3 × 50 back, 25 breast	
	3 × 50 breast, 25 free	
	3 × 50 free, 25 fly	
50	Free	
	Easy	
200	I.M.	
	For time	
200	Fly kick	Rest :15 between
150	Back kick	distances
100	Breast kick	
50	Free kick	
50	Fly pull with buoy	
100	Back pull with buoy	
150	Breast pull with buoy	
200	Free pull with buoy	
12 × 50	3 × 25 fly, 25 back	On 1:00 (:20)
	3 × 25 back, 25 breast	
	3 × 25 breast, 25 free	
	3 × 25 free, 25 fly	
5:00	Practice back turns	
200	Free	Swim-down

3,450 yards + 5:00 turn practice total

TAPER TRAINING

The taper is the third and final phase of your swimming season. During the taper comes the culmination of your strategy, discipline, and effort; the time when you will allow your body to rest and come to its full strength and sharpness for your race; the time when you will swim the fastest, but spend the least time in the water. Think of it as the icing on your cake or, if your prefer, the sparkle in your wine.

The fact is that daily training, if you're serious in your efforts, does take its toll, although at times you may not be as aware of it as others. In fact, serious training does *not* give you a feeling of increased energy daily; it may even give you a feeling of decreased energy. Rather, it gives you increased energy seasonally. So if decreased energy is the toll, then the increased energy following the taper is the reward. It's the old story of delayed gratification.

A taper is not the same as a mere rest. If it were, you could probably do it in no more than half the time. Again, you must delay your gratification just a little longer.

As the word *taper* suggests, during this time your training load drops off gradually. Exactly how much it drops off and how quickly depends on a number of variables. First, it depends on how tired you are from your midseason training and therefore how fast you'll recover. This can vary vastly from one individual to another, just as one person requires eight hours of sleep a night while another does fine on five. Second, it depends on how much training you've been doing per session and for how long. Generally, the more work you've done, the longer you'll need to taper. Third, it depends on the race distance you'll be doing. During the final week, sprinters will most likely taper down to a shorter workout distance than a distance swimmer will. Finally, the biggest determinant of the structure of a taper is probably the unique nature of each swimmer.

Unfortunately only experience can give you the answers you need to determine how much you should reduce your training. Face it, tapering is at best a series of educated guesses. In my experience as a coach, the tendency is more often to do too much, thereby preventing the body from reaching its full physiological peak, than to do too little. Adding to this is a psychological dimension. The swimmers who have worked the longest and hardest need the greatest amount of rest, but they almost always are the least willing to taper. They've gotten to where they are through hard work, and they feel the only way to go even further or to hold on to what they have is to work some more. Fortunately, the higher the level of your conditioning, the longer and more effectively you will be able to hold the peak of a taper.

If you haven't worked long enough or hard enough to develop any kind of long-term fatigue, don't taper. It's a loss of valuable training time, and it won't have the desired physiological effect.

For maximum benefit, the taper should cover about three weeks. This is not to be confused with reducing your training yardage for a day or two before a meet so as to experience a partial resting. The first week should consist of about 75 percent of your usual yardage with a trend toward reducing the number of swims in a set and increasing the rest interval so quality is heightened. But you should intersperse significant periods of moderate swimming between these quality swims.

During the second week, the amount of your training should gradually decrease to about 50 percent of normal, in approximately the same proportions as in the first week. Since your swimming time has been greatly reduced, you can spend some extra time practicing starts and turns.

The third week typically includes a long warm-up, a few fast swims at a race pace, and a thorough swim-down. At this point, you'll be doing only about 25 percent of your usual workout distance. Again, don't be afraid to do too little or even stay out of the water altogether if you feel like it. At the end of a taper, 20-minute workouts are not unusual. After all, you want to be sure that you don't leave your race in the pool before you arrive at the meet.

In short, the purpose of a taper is to sharpen your swimming after lengthy conditioning and development of skills. Don't worry if you feel somewhat sluggish initially during your taper, since the body when peaking sometimes needs a little time to adjust to a significantly lightened work load. Also, it's a good idea to discontinue the use of training devices (except for a pull buoy and a kickboard) and strength-building land exercises (but not stretching) during the taper.

Following are five typical taper workouts: a speed and a distance workout for week 1, a speed and a distance workout for week 2, and a workout for the end of week 3.

Week 1—Sprint

WORKOUT 51

Distance	Stroke	Time
200	Choice of strokes kick	Warm-up
200	Choice of strokes pull	
200	Choice of strokes swim	
300	I.M. Kick 2nd 25 of each stroke (no board) 3rd 25 faster than 1st 25	
3 × 100	Free broken #1: 75/25 #2: 50/50 #3: 50/25/25	Each break :10 Rest 2:00 between 100s
300	Free pull with buoy	
3 × 100	Your specialty broken #1: 75/25 #2: 50/50 #3: 50/25/25	Each break :10 Rest 2:00 between 100s
200	Free Easy	
8 × 25	1 hard, 1 easy each stroke	
300	Free	Swim-down
2,500	yards total	

Week 1—Endurance

WORKOUT 52

Distance	Stroke	Time
400	Free: Moderate	Warm-up
400	Free: At 1,000 free pace	
4 × 50	Free At pace you will be doing a free event	On 1:30
500	Free broken 200/100/100/100	Each break :10
200	I.M. kick	Rest :30 between
200	Free kick	200s
500	Free broken 200/100/50/50/50/50	Each break :10
400	Free	Swim-down
10:00	Practice dives	

2,800   yards + 10:00 dive practice total

Week 2—Sprint

━━━━━ WORKOUT 53 ━━━━━

Distance	Stroke	Time
400	Free Swim each 100 progressively faster	Warm-up
8 × 50	Free Breathe every 6 strokes	On 1:00
2 × 100	Your specialty Race pace from starting block	Rest 3:00 between 100s
400	Free pull with buoy Alternate 25 hard, 25 easy	
2 × 100	Your specialty broken #1: 50/50 #2: 25/25/25/25 From starting block	All breaks :10 Rest 3:00 between 100s
2 × { 75 50 25	Increase speed as distance decreases	Rest :20 after each distance
200	Free	Swim-down
10:00	Practice turns	

2,100   yards + 10:00 turn practice total

Week 2—Endurance

WORKOUT 54

Distance	Stroke	Time
400	I.M. reverse order 50 kick (no board), 50 swim each stroke	Warm-up
6 × 50	Free Baton, breathing every 6 strokes	On 1:10
500	Free 2 × 200 + 100 or your specialty (whichever is your event) Descend 100s Quick turns	Rest 2:00 betweens 200s and 100
500	Combination kick, pull with buoy Choice of strokes Your Choice	
4 × 25	Your specialty Very fast No breath From starting block	On 1:00
200	Free	Swim-down
2,000	yards total	

Week 3

WORKOUT 55

Distance	Stroke	Time
10:00	Choice of strokes	Warm-up
200	I.M. Alternate 25 kick (no board), 25 swim Moderate pace	
4 × 50	Your specialty At pace of a race you're swimming From starting block	Rest 1:00 between 50s
200	Free Easy	
8 × 12½	Your specialty Faster than race pace From starting block	Rest 1:00 between swims
200	Free	Swim-down
900	yards + 10:00 swim total	

8
FLEXIBILITY, STRENGTH, AND RESISTANCE

The idea of supplementing swimming with carefully selected nonswimming exercises for building flexibility or strength is not a new one, but it has played an increasingly important part in today's swim training programs. It makes training time more efficient, since you can develop strength and flexibility to higher levels more quickly by spending an extra 15–30 minutes a day three to five times a week doing land drills than by adding a lot more swimming. When I was training before the 1968 Olympics, I remember doing some land work, but very little compared to today's standards. The exercises we did 20 years ago were much less specific to swimming than those in use today.

My personal theory is that as swimmers become faster and faster, the answer to becoming still faster cannot continue to be swimming more and more and more, or we would soon be going round the clock. The answer must lie in efficient training outside the pool and outside of swimming—not as a substitute, but as a supplement. And therein is the value of land exercises that build flexibility or strength.

BUILDING FLEXIBILITY

The advantages of increased flexibility are many. Some of the more obvious ones follow:

- Increased flexibility means increased range of motion, which in turn means less resistance to movement, so motions require less energy.
- A stretched muscle contracts more quickly.
- Increased range of motion will improve alignment and stroke balance, thereby allowing for a more efficient stroke.
- A stretched muscle is less prone to injury.

Stretching is an excellent addition to any training program. It has the greatest short-term benefit when you do it immediately before swimming. You can also use stretching with reasonable effectiveness as a substitute for an in-the-water warm-up before an open water swim in which the water is cold enough that the chilling effect of immersion before the race would stiffen rather than loosen the muscles.

When doing a stretch, you must not "bounce" or force the stretch. Your movements should be slow and smooth, and you should not experience pain. Stop the movement of a stretch just short of pain and hold for at least 10–20 seconds.

The following stretching exercises contribute to good swimming. There are many others, so invent some for yourself.

SHOULDERS AND ARMS

Chicken Wings: Raise one elbow directly over your head, allowing your forearm to hang down your back. Push the elbow down behind your head with your other hand. Repeat with the other arm.

Doorway Stretch: Stand sideways, at arm's length just outside a doorway and reach back, placing your palm at shoulder height against the door sill. Keeping your arm straight, lean in to the doorway, moving your feet over for balance if necessary. Repeat with the other arm. Having a partner pull both arms toward each other at shoulder height behind your back works even better.

Arm Circles: Swing one arm forward in circles, keeping it straight. Repeat with the other arm.

Lateral Stretch: Extend one elbow directly in front of you, allowing the hand to rest on the opposite shoulder. Place the opposite hand on the back of your arm, and push the elbow toward the supporting shoulder with the opposite hand. Repeat with the other arm.

Towel Stretch: With your hands in front of you more than shoulder width apart, grasp a towel. Slowly rotate your straight arms backward over your head until your hands are behind your hips. Then slowly return to the starting position. As you become more flexible, move your hands closer together.

LEGS AND ANKLES

Thigh Stretch: Use one hand to hold on to a stationary object for support. With the other hand, grasp the top of the foot on the same side and pull it up toward the buttocks. Push the foot forward, stretching the thigh. Repeat with the other foot.

Wall Push-up: Place your palms against a wall, and your feet, toes pointing forward, 2–3 feet from the wall. If you're tall, you'll need to stand farther back. Keeping your heels on the floor, bend your elbows so your head nearly touches the wall. Return to the starting position. For greater stretching, try placing your toes on top of a thick book.

Plantar Sit: Kneel on a soft surface with the soles of your feet up, and sit back on your heels. Using your hands for balance, lean back and raise your knees off the floor as far as you can. Do not attempt this exercise if you have any knee soreness.

Hurdle Stretch: Sit with one leg extended straight in front of you, toes pointing up. Place the other ankle just above the straightened knee. Grab the farther foot with both hands, and try to touch your forehead to the point where your legs cross. Repeat with the other leg.

Yoga Sit: Sit with the soles of your feet together, your feet as close to your body as possible. Bend forward, trying to touch your forehead to your instep.

SPINE AND ABDOMEN

Front Extension: Lie on your stomach, and clasp your hands behind your head. Raise your shoulders and arms as high off the floor as possible.

Airplane Twists: Lie on your back with your arms spread at right angles to your body. Keeping your right foot in place, bring your left foot, leg straight, over to your right hand. Repeat with your right foot.

Quarter Sit-ups: Lie on your back with your knees bent, your feet about 12 inches from your hips. Cross your arms on your chest, and sit up to 45 degrees. Return to the starting position. Repeat.

Side Stretch: Stand with your arms extended overhead, hands clasped with palms facing each other. Lean to the right side as far as possible. Repeat on the left side.

Knee Curls: Lie on your back and grab your right knee. Pull it into your chest as you lift your upper body to meet it. Repeat with your left knee.

BUILDING STRENGTH

The most recent research into using nonswimming exercises to build strength in swimming concludes that just as in swimming, specificity in training is critical. In fact, not only must strength training simulate the movements of swimming, but it must also be performed at swimming speed. In other words, overall muscular power is not an asset to swimming unless it relates specifically to the stroke performed. Furthermore, general muscular strength, particularly the type requiring short, bulky muscles, can even be a detriment to swimming performance.

Additional strength can enhance efficiency and speed if the exercises meet the following criteria:

• They closely simulate swimming movements.

- They do not encourage compromises in stroke mechanics or stroke speed.
- They can be performed against greater resistance than that encountered by normal swimming.
- They can be adjusted to meet the demands of increasing strength.
- They minimize risk of injury.

Some strength-building equipment does meet these standards. Swimmers have successfully used the biokinetic swim bench, the Mini-Gym, elastic bands, pulleys, the Universal Gym, barbells, and Nautilus equipment.

BIOKINETIC SWIM BENCH

Of all the exercise equipment on the market, the biokinetic swim bench does the best job of allowing the user to duplicate swimming motions and stresses and provides the most information about the work being done. You can simulate the arm motions of all four strokes with this device. It is, however, costly.

The swim bench. (This one is not biokinetic.)

The reason for its effectiveness is that it is "isokinetic." This means that it uses the principle that if the resistance working against a moving object (such as a hand) is equal to the force being exerted in the opposite direction, the object will continue to move at a constant speed. The swimmer applies this principle by lying down on the bench in swimming position and pulling on two paddles attached to ropes that offer resistance. A digital readout tells how much resistance from the machine will counteract the force of the swimmer's pull. For maximum specificity, base the number of pulls and the duration of your exercise on how many strokes you need to complete a particular event in the goal time.

The biokinetic swim bench offers several advantages:

- Because of the isokinetic nature of this device, the amount of resistance is not limited by the weakest point of the stroke; as much strength building can take place at the strongest point as at the weakest. This is considerably more efficient than the strength building that takes place during swimming.
- The bench adjusts automatically to the strong and weak points of the individual rather than to predetermined limitations on "normal" range of motion.
- It duplicates closely a horizontal swimming position.
- It is well suited to high-speed training.
- It automatically adjusts to fatiguing so that the risk of injury is reduced.
- A strong swimmer and a weak swimmer can exercise with the same device and receive the same training benefit without having to adjust any controls.

MINI-GYM

The resistance mechanism of a Mini-Gym™ is similar to that of the biokinetic swim bench. The difference is that the Mini-Gym is not electronic and is one small unit about a foot square with a resistance rope and handle. It must be mounted on the wall or the floor, or two units can be mounted on a swim bench. A Mini-Gym lacks a digital readout but is less costly than a swim bench.

The Mini-Gym allows you many of the advantages of the biokinetic swim bench, but with some added versatility. A Mini-Gym, for example, can be mounted on the wall for use in lat pulls (extending the arms overhead and pulling and then pushing the hands down, bending the elbows, to waist level). When mounted on the floor, with the rope coming up behind you to shoulder height, it can even be used to develop the leg strength needed for hard push-offs from the wall. Suggestions on exercises that apply to swimming come with the purchase of a Mini-Gym.

ELASTIC BANDS

From an 8- to 10-foot length of half-inch surgical tubing, you can make a useful device by folding over each end and fastening it with tape to form handles. Wrap the center several times around a doorknob or other stationary object, hold on to the handles, and position a bench so that when you lie down with your arms over your head, the band is almost taut. (Standing with your upper body bent forward at a right angle will also work but may hurt your back.)

From this position, you can go through swimming motions at high speed. Be sure to go through the full range of motion on each arm cycle, even though tension will be greatest at the end of the pull phase and you may want to cut the stroke short. You can also throw the bands over the top of a door and use them for lat pulls, but watch out for the same tendency not to complete the pull.

As with the biokinetic swim bench, plan your sets of repetitions to correspond with the number of strokes you need for a specific event. The time required to do these repetitions will probably be less because your hands can move faster than when in the water.

This rapid hand speed, while it's a benefit in training, is one of the two major drawbacks of using elastic bands to build strength. Because of the speed, shoulder strain is high and you can develop tendonitis, so be careful and cut back at the slightest sign of shoulder pain. The second drawback is that, for the portions of the stroke where resistance is the lowest, no significant training effect is taking place. You can adjust resistance by moving the bench closer to or farther from the point at which the bands are attached, but if you are to be able to complete each stroke, tension at the beginning of the pull will always be too low.

The advantages of elastic bands are that you can use them almost anywhere and they cost very little. You may wish to wear gloves to avoid blisters.

PULLEYS

A pulley device is simply a rope with a handle at one end, a weight at the other end, and a fixed pulley in the middle. When you grasp the handle, the rope forms a right angle, the weight or weights resting on the floor. Pulleys are used in pairs, one for each arm. Commercial models have interchangeable weights for varying needs. You can also make your own, using bricks or cans filled with sand or concrete for weights and two eye bolts or pulleys attached to a wall.

With pulleys, as with other equipment, lying on a bench most closely simulates the swimming position.

One disadvantage of pulleys is that your stroke turnover will probably be slower than in the water. If the weight is low enough that you can achieve rapid turnover, the ballistic effect of the weights traveling quickly will lower resistance, diminishing the training benefit. Another disadvantage is that your hands do not travel at a constant speed as with isokinetic equipment.

Pulleys, like elastic bands, can be used almost anywhere. If you make your own, the cost is minimal.

UNIVERSAL GYM

Universal Gym™ is the name given to a system of stationary weights, as opposed to barbells, which are considered "free" weights. Although weights in general are poorly suited to swim training because they slow down body movements, a Universal Gym offers more options than free weights, is safer to use because nothing can fall on you, and adjusts quickly and easily to offer varying amounts of resistance.

A Universal Gym is a large and costly contraption not suitable for home use. Among its options are several devices for leg press and leg extension. This is a plus, since many strength-building devices ignore the legs. Also, one station has a bar you can hang from and lift your legs to build abdominal strength. With the many stations available on a Universal Gym, part of the challenge is to do only those exercises which build swimming strength. Bench presses, for example, will do nothing to improve your swimming. Fortunately, since Universal Gyms are found mainly at recreation facilities, schools, and health clubs, someone is usually available to instruct you in the proper and appropriate use of the apparatus.

In general, keep the weight at a level where your repetitions can be fairly rapid and numerous. Supplement your weight training with one of the forms of strength training that allows for faster movement.

BARBELLS

Of all the strength-training equipment discussed so far, barbells are the least effective in terms of duplicating swimming movements. They are, however, inexpensive if you make them yourself. You can do this easily by using a pipe that is four feet long (120 cm) and one to two inches (2.4–4.8 cm) in diameter, and two 48 ounce cans. Fill the pipe and the cans with ready-mix concrete, and push the pipe into the cans. You will then have a barbell that weighs about 21 pounds (9.5 kg).

You can do some reasonably effective exercises lying on your back (be sure to bend your knees). Extend your arms behind your head, and lift the barbell up about 1½ feet off the floor. Also, you can stand, supporting the barbell on your shoulders, and duplicate with your legs the pushing-off-the-wall motion of a turn by bending and straightening your legs.

NAUTILUS EQUIPMENT

Nautilus™ is the name of the largest and most sophisticated system of stationary weights on the market. The name comes from a cam device that is an integral part of the system and is shaped like a nautilus shell. This cam varies the resistance you encounter with the degree of contraction of your muscles as you go through a particular range of motion.

With ordinary weights or with the Universal Gym, you can press or lift only as much weight as the weakest area of your full range can tolerate. This means that during much of your range, the training benefit is limited and you must therefore do many repetitions. With Nautilus, you can tax a muscle fully throughout an exercise because resistance is highest at the muscle's strongest point and lowest at its weakest (although the machine doesn't compensate for individual differences). In other words, Nautilus equipment provides an isokinetic form of exercise so efficient that fewer repetitions are required than with a Universal Gym.

The problem is that Nautilus equipment is specifically designed to be used at slow speeds and therefore is of limited value to swimmers, especially when considering that the cost of using such equipment, usually found only in health clubs, is considerable. If you use it at all, use it only during the earliest part of the season, and do more rapid exercises after that.

CREATING A CIRCUIT

Creating a "circuit" of different exercises with different pieces of equipment arranged in stations has worked well for many teams. Perhaps the reason for this success is that such a setup can include some exercises done at very high rates, which improve sprinting ability, as well as some done at moderately high rates, which improve endurance. The value in diversity is that few swimmers specialize in just one event, and the circuit allows several swimmers to train at the same time.

At stations done at sprint speed, gradually work up to

four sets of 30-60 repetitions, resting :30-:45 between sets. At stations emphasizing endurance (except when using Nautilus equipment), gradually increase up to four sets of 20-40 repetitions, resting :30-:45 or more between sets. If you experience any pain at all, by all means *do less*.

BUILDING FLEXIBILITY AND STRENGTH IN THE WATER

Flexibility and strength training need not be reserved strictly for dry land. Some helpful approaches in the water include the use of various training devices and some exercises involving swimming movements. The training devices described here are those used in the workouts in this book. (For a description of the devices themselves, see the Glossary.)

Training devices

FINS

Swim fins are excellent for helping you develop a feel for the water with your feet. Because of the large surface area of the fins, your kicks will exert more pressure on the water, which will in turn create more resistance against your feet. You will feel this pressure, but the real benefit is that this resistance stretches the toes farther from the ankles, thereby increasing flexibility. It is likely, too, that since your leg muscles must push down a larger "foot" during the propulsive phase of the kick, your legs are developing more strength with the fins.

Fins are particularly useful as an aid to learning the stroke technique used in butterfly. They develop extra power and undulating motion, which help you get your arms out of the water at the end of each stroke.

In backstroke, fins can help you gain and maintain body position.

Swim fins are an excellent aid to butterfly training.

HAND PADDLES

Hand paddles are excellent for strengthening shoulder, chest, and back muscles. The reason is the increased resistance of pulling a larger "hand" through the water. If you use paddles during pulling, your heart rate will increase because of the added resistance. You will also add stress to a pulling series. But since too much work can cause soreness, ease into your use of paddles and take care not to overdo it.

KICKBOARD

A kickboard is invaluable in building leg strength, because you can transfer to your legs all the stress of moving the body forward. This can also rapidly bring on a high heart rate, because the heart must pump a tremendous volume of blood to the large muscles that are farthest from it. Leg strength contributes significantly to the power needed for fast sprints and is crucial to a hard finish at the end of a race. In addition, a strong kick is needed to maintain good body position.

With a kickboard, you can also isolate the legs from the rest of the stroke so that you can concentrate solely on kicking motions while maintaining body position.

PULL BUOY

Used alone, a pull buoy may slightly increase the stress on the arms, but the real benefit comes from using it in conjunction with one or more other devices. Swimmers often combine a pull buoy with hand paddles and a small inner tube around the ankles. You can also use it with the equipment discussed later under Additional Training Devices. Or use a pull buoy to isolate the arms so you can concentrate your attention on the armstroke.

Pull buoy, paddles, tube, and kickboard are excellent devices for improving strength and flexibility.

TUBE

By putting a small scooter-size inner tube around your ankles during pulling, you will be adding resistance to your pulling. This will strengthen your shoulder, chest, and back muscles, just as through the use of hand paddles. For maximum benefit, use a tube in conjunction with hand paddles and a pull buoy.

You will probably find that using a tube decreases your speed significantly. One reason is the resistance. In addition, there is a tendency to kick slightly when using only a pull buoy; once encircled by a tube, your feet will be unable to move.

ADDITIONAL RESISTANCE DEVICES

Other resistance devices come in all shapes and sizes and include vests or suits with cuplike pockets to catch water, gloves with webbing between the fingers, wrist weights to wear while swimming, and kickboards with scoops on the bottom. Also, practicing while wearing two and even three bathing suits has become popular since the appearance in 1974 of tight Lycra "skin" suits for competition. Some swimmers have even gone so far as to wear clothing such as T-shirts or shorts to create drag during their training sessions so as to feel like greased lightning in a race when they wear only a tight-fitting bathing suit.

The following strength-building exercises are designed to be done in the water. All but one of them require no equipment.

Feet-First Breaststroke: Position your body in a right angle with your hips down in the water and your ankles and ears above the surface. Propulsion comes from taking small breaststroke pulls at your sides so that your body moves forward feet first. This is a good way to strengthen your abdominal muscles and your triceps.

Head-Out Freestyle: Swim freestyle for short sprints with your head out, focusing your eyes on a point directly in front of you and keeping your head still. This exercise is useful in developing leg strength, since your legs must work harder to stay near the surface when your head is up so high.

152

Head-out freestyle

Press-Ups: Begin by placing your hands, shoulder width apart, flat on the edge of the pool while allowing your body to rest vertically in deep water. (If water deeper than your height isn't available, try bending your knees in shallower water.) Press your body out of the water until your elbows are straight. Return to the starting position. You may wish to drape a towel over the edge of the pool to avoid abrasion to your wrists and the front of your suit.

Try doing press-ups in sets of 10 or 20 at a time and then work up, but do no more than you can do without interrupting a continuous up-and-down motion. This will enable you to develop the strength necessary for a strong stroke finish. Discontinue press-ups if you develop any wrist pain.

Tethered Swimming: You will need an 18- to 20-foot (6-meter) length of half-inch (1.2-cm) surgical tubing, and a sturdy, wide canvas belt. Fasten the belt around your waist. Make a loop at each end of the tubing, and slide the belt through it. Wrap the middle of the tubing several times around a ladder, pole, or other stationary object near the edge of the pool. Then swim out from the edge as far as the tubing will allow, and keep stroking powerfully to avoid slipping backward. Hold your position for a particular number of strokes or a certain length of time, based on the time required for your specialty event.

Many commercial models of this device are available. They may be more comfortable, more convenient, or more durable, but basically the principle is the same. You may want to buy such a device, since it offers some distinct training advantages, especially when you must train in a small pool.

Vertical Kicking: Kick with a breaststroke or eggbeater kick (a breaststroke kick with one leg at a time) in a completely vertical position with your hands on top of your head. It is most beneficial to remain absolutely vertical if you can, since leaning forward or backward allows your natural buoyancy to assist you.

The higher out of the water you can bring your body with the force of your kick, the greater the strength-building benefit. My suggestion for a pattern of work and rest is to kick for :30, rest for :15, and repeat this pattern for 3:00 or more.

9
OPEN WATER SWIMMING

Until five or six years ago, I thought that being surrounded on all four sides by pool walls was the only way to swim. I am astounded at my lack of imagination when I think that I spent three of my most serious years of swim training in Fort Lauderdale, Florida, where the ocean temperature is unusually palatable. But I suppose the real problem was not so much lack of imagination as it was that I had never heard of an open water race except on the professional circuit (I once met Abou Heif of Egypt), so, of course, I'd never come across anyone who had done one.

Since then, I've grown to view an open water swim as the ultimate swimming experience. I love the freedom, the gratification of moving continuously in the same direction, and the ever-expanding depth of blue. Also, I enjoy the festivity of a picnic afterward in scenic surroundings and the camaraderie of friends experiencing postcompetition exhilaration.

But the feeling that becomes postcompetition camaraderie can, if you let it, be an early-competition nightmare titled "Where Did All These Crazy People Come From?" I mean, who else but crazy people would thrash their arms and legs wildly through the foam, all to gain access to the three square feet of water directly around me? No one ever made such a fuss to get this close before! Is it possible that the water temperature has done permanent brain damage to all these human piranhas?

MENTAL PREPARATION

If this is a familiar scenario, or even if it's one you've only worried about, you're not alone. In fact, you've probably hit on the two greatest causes of fear in open water swimming: cold water and crowds of swimmers during the first part of the race. However, adding some mental preparation to your physical conditioning will bolster your confidence. As an aid to your mental preparation, consider the following points:

- Since water acts as a cushion, any blow from another swimmer's arm or leg is far less likely to hurt you than merely to cause a temporary loss of concentration.
- Other swimmers don't get in your way on purpose, so don't feel offended. Running into you slows them down as much as it does you, and frequently it's difficult to see, much less to find room.
- If you are particularly concerned about the thrashing arms and legs of other swimmers, you can always take your time at the start. You can position yourself at the back of the pack before going in the water, and if there are buoys to be rounded, go wide. Most swimmers want the shortest, fastest route, so the farther back and the wider you go, the less competition you'll have.
- If your strength and stamina are good, you can position yourself at the front of the pack before takeoff and sprint out ahead of the crowd. But do this only if you are an experienced, well-conditioned swimmer who won't be exhausted by this technique and who won't get in the way of other swimmers coming from behind.
- Remember that you can swim with filled or poorly positioned goggles, so if they are knocked askew by another swimmer, keep swimming until you are in the

156

clear before you roll over on your back to adjust them. In fresh water, you may want to avoid this problem by going without goggles altogether.

- Even in swims with close to a thousand participants, the crowd thins relatively quickly. Whatever problems you may have with the proximity of other swimmers are short-lived.

- If the water is cold, you may experience a gasping sensation when you first enter the water, especially if you're in a triathlon and are heated up from running or biking. This usually occurs only when anxiety is high, however, so the best antidote is to relax and breathe deeply. Also, even if you don't actually immerse yourself in the water before the race, at least wade around and splash some water on your arms and shoulders so you are mentally more prepared for immersion.

- If the cold particularly bothers you, try swimming with your head out until your breathing and stroke feel relatively comfortable. However, this technique will slow you down and requires extra effort.

Once you've overcome the challenges of "all those crazy people" at the beginning of your swim, you may feel quite the opposite in the middle of it. You may begin to feel that you're all alone out there and can't even see the bottom. At such times, I sometimes fantasize that I'm beating everyone, including all the men. But, seriously, this can be a lonely feeling. To make matters worse, you may be running into cold spots or debris floating in the water.

At times like these, simply say to yourself, "Don't panic!" Realize that you are among the elements, and the environment is less controlled than in the pool. It may help to concentrate on some of the same things you concentrate on in the pool: proper stroke technique, consistent rhythm, complete exhalation, and the like. Probably the greatest comfort is a sense of confidence about your own preparation and your own physical ability.

GAINING A PHYSICAL ADVANTAGE

In addition to training for open water swims, observe the following guidelines for help with your physical preparation for open water swimming.

- Always do some form of warm-up before swimming hard. If the water is uncomfortably cold, say below 62 degrees, you may want to do some stretching and a little jogging on the beach to elevate body temperature. If you can tolerate it, go in the water and swim out at least 200–300 yards and get a feel for the temperature or any unusual characteristics of the bottom. Then turn around and look at the finish line (if you finish in the same place as you start). Decide what landmarks to look for as you're coming in at the end of the race.
- As you swim back in to shore, notice how far out you are when the bottom becomes visible, and how the bottom looks at the point where you should stand up to run in to the finish line. This will also give you an idea how far to run out at the beginning of the race.
- Before race day, practice running out from shore through shallow water and submerging by diving headlong when the water reaches midthigh. If the water remains shallow for a long distance, try doing several headlong dives in rapid succession, pushing off from the bottom after each one.
- Since the technique of sprinting out in front of the crowd, as mentioned, has its advantages, practice swimming the fastest part of your interval sets in the pool first, rather than descending your swims. When you do practice swims in open water, do the first 200–300 yards of your swim hard before you settle into your pace.
- In practice, work on breathing on both sides so that during a race you can watch for landmarks on either side. This also enables you to breathe away from waves rolling from one side.

- Practice going under rather than through any large oncoming waves.
- Lifting your head during breathing wastes time and energy, but it is necessary to some degree when trying to stay on course during an open water swim. Choose your landmarks carefully, the taller the better, so that they can be seen with the least alteration in normal breathing movements. Train yourself to limit raising your head to once every 8–10 strokes and to pick out reliable swimmers to follow in a race so that you can get away with looking even less. (At times, you may want to aim deliberately to the side of a landmark or course marker to compensate for currents.)
- You may even want to practice "drafting" off another swimmer who swims at your speed. To do this, swim as closely behind the other person as you can without touching. You will conserve energy and perhaps avoid looking so frequently for landmarks.

SAFETY GUIDELINES

In your desire to prepare yourself mentally and physically for the open water experience, don't overlook the importance of safety. Personal safety is critical in open water, when assistance may be a good deal farther away than in a pool situation. Open water also presents more hazards than are to be found around a pool. The following points will help you plan your swims with safety in mind so that you can experience maximum enjoyment:

- **Never swim alone**, no matter how well trained you are. You do not have control over weather, water temperature, boat traffic, and a myriad of other factors. If you can't find anyone skilled or courageous to swim with you, stay close to shore and have someone watch you from there.
- Begin your open water experience gradually with relatively short periods of immersion in water of moderate

temperature and with at least one experienced swimmer as a companion. Be sure you understand where you're going and what to look for before you start. And by all means, **don't start if you have any doubts about your ability to finish**.

- Be careful about boat traffic. Just as the drivers of cars are not always on the lookout for something as small as a bicycle, the drivers of boats are seldom on the lookout for swimmers—in fact, even less so. Your best protection is to swim where boats are prohibited (although sometimes no such area exists). Wear an orange cap—the universal color of warning.

- For protection against hypothermia, wear two caps, the heavier the better. As much as 30 percent of the body heat you lose is through your head. Some swimmers coat small hunks of lamb's wool with Vaseline and insert them in their ears to help reduce heat loss.

- For open water swims that require long immersion in very cold water, you can also control heat loss by putting a layer of lanolin (available in pharmacies) on your skin. In addition, lanolin can prevent rubbing and chafing of the skin at the seams of women's suit straps.

- Consuming even moderate amounts of alcohol within three days before an open water event will make you more sensitive to cold.

- Learn to release a cramp in your calf by turning your toes up toward your knees to stretch the muscle. For cramps in other areas, float on your stomach and stretch or massage the muscle in any way you can.

WORKOUTS FOR OPEN WATER SWIMMING

The joys of swimming in the open water can be great, but especially when safety is an important consideration, nothing beats the pool for conditioning. If you think for a moment about some of the training principles discussed ear-

lier, you'll understand why. High-intensity interval training requires precisely defined distances and consistent
water conditions, both of which are available only in a
pool. The aspects of open water swimming that make it an
exciting relief from the monotony of pool swimming—the
wide-open spaces, the oneness with nature—make it less
suitable for everyday training.

Some adaptations to your pool workouts will make them
more applicable to building skills useful in open water
swimming. First, since racing in the open water usually
requires some hard sprinting at the start to get away from
the crowd, make the first swim (or swims if they are short)
the fastest rather than the slowest as in a descending set.
Second, consider building your swimming sets around
quarter-mile, half-mile, and full-mile increments instead of
around distances found in pool competition. The reason
for this is that most open water swims are measured in
miles, not yards. Third, emphasize endurance freestyle
work. You may even want to consider doing greater total
workout distances because the shortest open water swims
are usually at least one mile (although triathlon swims may
be less), whereas the longest pool event is just under one
mile. The following workouts, intended for use in training
in a pool for open water swimming, have been constructed
with these concepts in mind.

WORKOUT 56

Distance	Stroke	Time
50	Free	Warm-up
100	Free kick	
150	Free pull	
200	Free	
50	Free pull with buoy, paddles, and	Rest :10 per 50
100	tube	between ech
150		distance
200		
200	Free: Get time	Rest 1:00 between
400	2 × 200 time + :5	each distance
600	400 time + 200 time + :5	
800	2 × 400 time	
200	Free kick	Rest :10 per 50
150		between each
100		distance
50		
9 × 50	Free	On 1:00 (:10)
	25 head-out, 25 normal	
200	Free	Swim-down
4,150	yards total	

WORKOUT 57

Distance	Stroke	Time
100	Free	Warm-up
	Get as much distance per stroke as possible	
100	Ripple	
100	Free	
	Count strokes and keep consistent count	
150	Free	
8 × 75	Free kick	On 1:30
50	Free	Rest :30 between
100	Lengthen out stroke as distance	swims
150	increases	
200		
250		
300		
350		
400		
3 × 300	Free pull with buoy, paddles, and tube	On 4:15 (:20)
200	Free	Swim-down
3,950	yards total	

WORKOUT 58

Distance	Stroke	Time
150	Free: Breathe on right	Warm-up
150	Free: Breathe on left	
150	Free: Alternate breathing	
9 × 50	Free baton	On :50 (:10)
	3 breathe on right	
	3 breathe on left	
	3 alternate breathing	
200	Free	Rest :30 between
300	I.M. broken	swims
	Break :10 at 75s	
400	Free	
200	I.M. broken	
	Break :10 at 50s	
600	Free	
100	I.M. broken	
	Break :10 at 25s	
9 × 50	Free kick	On 1:00
3 × 150	Free	On 2:15 (:20)
	#1: Breathe on right	
	#2: Breathe on left	
	#3: Alternate breathing	
200	Free	Swim-down
3,800	yards total	

WORKOUT 59

Distance	Stroke	Time
10:00	Choice of strokes	Warm-up
4 × 75	Free 25 right arm, 25 left arm, 25 normal	On 1:20 (:15)
2 × 150	Alternate 25 ripple, 25 normal	On 2:15 (:20)
300	Even pace	
8 × 75	Free: 1st 25 fastest	On 1:15 (:10)
4 × 150	1st 50 fastest	On 2:15 (:20)
2 × 300	1st 100 fastest	On 4:15 (:30)
300	Free pull with buoy, paddles, and tube	
2 × 150	Free pull with buoy and paddles	On 2:15 (:20)
4 × 75	Free pull with buoy	On 1:15 (:15)
100	Free	Swim-down

3,700   yards + 10:00 swim total

━━ WORKOUT 60 ━━

Distance	Stroke	Time
200	Free Alternate breathing Alternate 25 head-out, 25 normal	Warm-up
12 × 150	Free 3 kick 3 swim 3 pull with buoy, paddles, and tube 3 swim	Rest :20 between 150s
6 × 75	25 fly, 25 back, 25 breast	On 1:30 (:20)
900	Free 1st 300 fastest	
100	Free	Swim-down
3,700	yards total	

GLOSSARY

Abbreviations used in workouts:
Back = Backstroke
Breast = Breaststroke
Fly = Butterfly
Free = Freestyle
I.M. = Individual Medley

Alternate breathing: Breathing alternately on the right and left sides during freestyle.

Around-the-walls: Starting swims in the middle of the pool rather than at the wall in order to obtain more practice on turns.

Backstroke flags: A line of usually colorful flags stretching across the width of the pool five yards from the pool wall at each end. The purpose of the flags is to help the swimmer anticipate turns.

Baton: Holding a short stick (6–8 inches long) in one hand as you take a freestyle stroke with the opposite arm. When the stroking arm returns to the forward position, the hand that was stationary grabs the baton, and the other arm takes a stroke. The process is then repeated.

Board: A rectangular piece of buoyant material large enough to give support to the arms during kicking drills, but small enough to handle easily during turns.

Broken swim: A swim in which one or more rest interval(s) are inserted.

167

Buoy: See Pull Buoy.

Catch-up: The method of swimming freestyle in which each arm completes one whole stroke, coming to rest in the forward position, before the other arm begins its cycle.

Descend: Doing a series of swims of equal distance, each faster than the preceding swim.

Drafting: Swimming directly behind another person, as close as possible without touching. This strategy conserves energy and is often used in open water swimming.

Eggbeater kick: A breaststroke kick alternating one leg at a time.

Endurance event: In this book, a swimming event of 200 yards or more.

Fists: Swimming freestyle (unless another stroke is specified) with hands in fists instead of with the palms flat.

Hand paddles: *See* Paddles.

Head-out: Swimming freestyle for short sprints with the head out, focusing on a point directly in front so the swimmer's head doesn't move from side to side.

Hesitation: Swimming freestyle, stopping arm motion when one arm is extended all the way forward and the other arm is all the way back. During this pause, which takes place after each stroke, the only propulsion is from the kick.

Individual medley: An event consisting of equal distances of butterfly, backstroke, breaststroke, and freestyle, in that order.

Interval training: A type of conditioning consisting of periods of submaximal exercise alternating with controlled, short rest periods. Interval swimming can involve beginning each set on a fixed departure time, or getting a fixed amount of rest between each set, or interspersing occasional easy paced lengths between sets.

Kickboard: *See* Board.

Negative split: The situation resulting when the second half of a swim is faster than the first.

Paddles: Plastic plates that come in various shapes and fit on the palms for the purpose of adding resistance and thereby building strength.

Pull buoy: A flotation device fitting partly below the thighs and partly above the thighs (in swimming position) with connective material in between. It is used for isolating the arms while still holding the legs up, without kicking, for the purpose of strength building or working on stroke technique.

Recovery: The portion of the stroke during which the arms and legs return to the position from which they begin propulsion.

Repeat: One swim in a series of swims of equal distance.

Ripple: A freestyle stroke in which the fingertips touch the surface of the water during the entire recovery phase, creating ripples on the surface.

Side kick: Kicking on the side with one arm extended under the head and the other arm extending along the top side.

Sprint event: A swimming event of 100 yards or less.

Starting block: A square platform at the end of the pool, not more than one meter from the surface of the water. This platform is used for out-of-the-water starts as well as for in-the-water starts.

Streamlining: The act of making the body as aquadynamic as possible by pointing the toes, straightening the elbows, keeping the head down, and in general creating as little resistance as possible.

Stroke: An arm cycle with either the right or the left arm; a complete armstroke with both arms constitutes two strokes.

Tube: A small scooter-size inner tube that wraps around the ankles to add resistance and build strength during pulling.

BIBLIOGRAPHY

Brems, M. "Backstroke Mini-Clinic." *Swim* (Dec./Jan. 1984): 33.

———. "Freestyle Mini-Clinic." *Swim* (Feb./March 1985): 36.

———. "Butterfly Mini-Clinic." *Swim* (June/July 1985): 30.

———. "Breaststroke Mini-Clinic." *Swim* (April/May 1985): 38.

———. *101 Favorite Swimming Workouts*. San Mateo, CA: Workouts, 1980.

———. *Swim for Fitness*. San Francisco: Chronicle Books, Inc., 1979.

———. *"The Fit Swimmer: 120 Workouts and Training Tips*. Chicago: Contemporary Books, Inc., 1984

Maglischo, E. W. *Swimming Faster: A Comprehensive Guide to the Science of Swimming*. Palo Alto, CA: Mayfield Publishing Co., 1982.

Thornton, N. "Training for the Future." *Swimming Technique* (May-July 1987): 11–14.

INDEX